# VICTOR

# VICTOR

## VICTOR TORRES
### WITH DON WILKERSON

WHITAKER
HOUSE

All Scripture quotations are taken from the *King James Version Easy Read Bible*, KJVER®, © 2001, 2007, 2010, 2015 by Whitaker House. Used by permission. All rights reserved.

## VICTOR

Thevictormovie.com

facebook.com/VictorTorresMinistries
newlifeforyouth.com

New Life Outreach International Church
P.O. Box 13526
Richmond, VA 23225

ISBN: 978-1-64123-053-7
eBook ISBN: 978-1-64123-054-4
Printed in the United States of America
© 2017 by Victor Torres

Whitaker House
1030 Hunt Valley Circle
New Kensington, PA 15068
www.whitakerhouse.com

**Library of Congress Cataloging-in-Publication Data**

Names: Torres, Victor, 1943– author. | Wilkerson, Don, author.
Title: Victor / by Victor Torres with Don Wilkerson.
Description: New Kensington, PA : Whitaker House, 2017. | Includes
   bibliographical references. |
Identifiers: LCCN 2017043857 (print) | LCCN 2017044139 (ebook) | ISBN
   9781641230544 (E-book) | ISBN 9781641230537 (trade pbk. : alk. paper)
Subjects: LCSH: Torres, Victor, 1943– | Drug addicts—New York (State)—New
   York—Biography. | Christian converts—New York (State)—New
   York—Biography. | Brooklyn (New York, N.Y.)—Biography. | New York
   (N.Y.)—Biography.
Classification: LCC BV4935.T65 (ebook) | LCC BV4935.T65 A3 2017 (print) |
   DDC 248.2 [B] —dc23
LC record available at https://lccn.loc.gov/2017043857

2  3  4  5  6  7  8  9  10  11  **ᗯ**  24  23  22  21  20  19  18  17

# DEDICATION

This book is dedicated to the glory of God and to my beloved parents for their persistent search toward a new life for their "lost but found" son. It is also dedicated to my wonderful wife and best friend, Carmen, and to our four children: Feliza, Rosalinda, Michelle, and Victor Phillip (Tito), whom I love dearly.

# ACKNOWLEDGEMENTS

I am ever grateful for the impact that David Wilkerson had upon my life. His calling, which led him to the mean streets of New York City and the Teen Challenge ministry, touched my life and provided a way for me to come to Christ and have a second chance in life. I am also thankful for Nicky Cruz who reached out to me and became a great model of inspiration and faith to believe God for my own miracle. He inspired me to dream big with God, and I am grateful for his leadership. His personal interest in me helped me go to Bible College and prepare for my calling.

I am also very grateful for Don Wilkerson who ministered to me since day one; when I was hurting and in doubt, struggling as a young Christian. He encouraged me and prayed for me while I went through the program at Teen Challenge. Throughout the years of my ministry, he has been instrumental with his great wisdom and advice to stay the course. Today Don is a member of the New Life for Youth Board of Directors. He and his wife, Cindy, continue to be a great source of encouragement and support to my ministry.

Also, I would like to thank Arlene Moskwa, my daughter Rosalinda Rivera, and Emily Lewis, for their assistance in preparing this special revised edition of my book.

You can contact me at www.newlife1.org or you can write to me at New Life Outreach International Church, P. O. Box 13526, Richmond, VA 23225.

# CONTENTS

# FOREWORD

When I first met Victor Torres, he was a junkie (a heroin addict), an outcast from society. Victor came to the center with his parents, who suffered greatly because of his condition. He was skinny, pale, and sick because his body needed heroin. He was just one of many like him from Puerto Rican families and the ghetto environment.

I was director of the Teen Challenge Center at the time Victor came to us. After we accepted him into our program, he went through the entire trauma so many drug addicts experience. He was tempted, divided in his mind, and his body ached with pain. Victor's torment brought our staff of ex-convicts and ex-drug addicts to our knees asking God for a miracle in this life so lost because of sin.

I remember the day God broke through to Victor's mind, his heart, and his very soul. I remember when love, peace, and joy infiltrated his life. He was lifted up into the place of God's forgiveness. He accepted Jesus with tears of gratitude. He gave his fears, insecurity, uncertainty, and loneliness to the Lord and the Lord took over.

What can I say about the Victor of today? Years have passed and Victor went on to college. He is now a mighty man of God living and ministering in Richmond, Virginia, with his wife, Carmen, and four children, Feliza, Rosalinda, Michelle, and son Victor Phillip. He takes his roles as husband and father very seriously.

I believe in the years to come you will hear much concerning this young man because the anointing of the Lord is in his life. Victor's credentials are not because he belongs to a well-respected denomination, but because he has a message for the parents and for the youth of this country. Besides, his credentials have approval from heaven.

The fruit of his ministry, New Life for Youth and New Life Outreach International Church, prove not only Victor's capabilities and his experience but also his genuine love for young people and the unity of the family.

As you read this book, you'll be right there in those tenement buildings. You'll feel the pain that Victor's family felt. You'll see what life in the ghetto was like in the '60's. I pray that this book will give you a burden, compassion, and sense of urgency because the fight against corruption, drug addiction, and crime in our communities is not over.

Pray for Victor and his ministry. Let this inspiring book be another reminder to you that God can take the "down-and-out" and give them self-respect while transforming them into servants of Jesus Christ of Nazareth.

And, remember, Jesus loves you.

—*Nicky Cruz*
Author, *Run Baby Run*

# INTRODUCTION

It was my privilege to first help Victor Torres write and publish this book in 1973. I was, at the time, Director of the Brooklyn Teen Challenge Center, founded by my brother David Wilkerson, author of *The Cross and the Switchblade*.

Victor entered our center in November 1963, a skinny, strung-out dope fiend.

His total transformation and rehabilitation from drugs and as a former gang member in Brooklyn's notorious "Brownsville" section in the latter 1950's and early 1960's is an incredible story of the grace, mercy, and power of God; saving Victor from either certain death, or a long-term prison sentence. Truly, Victor lived on "Evil Street."

Why tell this story again?

Because one only has to read today's headlines or look around where you live to see that the history of gangs and drugs is being repeated with a vengeance.

Teenage gangs have risen up again in major urban centers, as well as in midsize cities and even small towns. In fact, rural America is no longer immune from the ravages of gangs and drugs. But today's gangs are armed to kill—with handguns, even automatic weapons, and other firepower. They are potentially ten times more dangerous than the gangs of the '50's and '60's. In those days, gangs inflicted their damage on other gangs. Today anyone who gets in the way can be a victim of a drive-by shooting or a crime. Juvenile crime has risen 50% from 1988 to 1992, and it continues to rise yearly.

In major cities, certain neighborhoods are not controlled by the police but by the "hoods." One gang in Chicago, the Gangsters Disciples, now have their own political agenda—to become a well-organized coalition to buy politicians and have influence on the government—and the laws.

Victor was a gang member of the "Roman Lords" of Brooklyn, New York. Were he a teenager today, he would be living in the same scene.

But he is not. He is now married and a father of four. Jesus Christ, by the work of the Holy Spirit, and through his mother's prayers, transformed him miraculously. Victor was then, and is still now, "born again" into a new life.

From that horror of addiction, Victor also was "set free" by the power of God through prayer.

I am so moved every time I tell even parts of Victor's life transformation that I encouraged him to reprint it, so readers could read the whole story and follow the saga from gang member, to narcotic addiction, to near death from drug withdrawal—to the man of God he is today.

I am a personal eyewitness to the exciting events that took place once he walked off "Evil Street" and entered the door of the Teen Challenge Center at 416 Clinton Avenue, Brooklyn, New York.

Every family member touched by drugs, alcohol, delinquency, or similar problems needs to read Victor's story and be challenged in faith, that God can do it again. If God could do it for Victor Torres, he can do it for anyone.

If you know a teen, youth, young adult, even an adult heading for trouble, I urge you, try to put this book into his or her hands.

If you know gang members, show them the title of the book —it may intrigue them enough to want to read it.

And if you know a drug addict—either on the streets, in prison, in a recovery program, or recently coming off drugs—this book is a blueprint for escaping "Evil Street" and finding one's way onto a street called "New Life."

We also encourage those who work with troubled teens, drug users, and abusers or others who can identify with the lifestyle Victor once lived— to purchase this book. Put it in the hands of all those currently living on "Evil Street," because this book may save their life. But, more importantly, it can show them how Jesus Christ can change their life and start them on a brand new road to freedom and peace.

Victor's story is the fulfillment of Jesus' words, *"Whom the Son has set free is free indeed"* (John 8:36).

—*Don Wilkerson*
Executive Director, Teen Challenge

# 1

# VICTOR

Mother ran into my room. I was lying on the floor beside my bed. A needle protruded out of my left arm. I was unconscious.

"My son, my son is dead! Oh God—he's dead!" my mother screamed hysterically.

Ricky, my younger brother, had just discovered my body on the floor. In panic, he screamed and ran for Mom. As she sobbed over my body, Ricky stood in the doorway crying.

That morning when I had awakened I was sick, so sick I couldn't get out of bed to go find the usual place where I took my morning fix … and my afternoon fix … and my evening fix (and sometimes a few in between).

"Ricky, come here!" I had yelled from the room. "I'm too sick to go out. Will you get my works (syringe) for me?" By now, Ricky was accustomed to his brother's drug routine. He even tried to get me, to stop talking to him like a big brother, though he was only a young kid.

"Get me a glass of water," I said as he handed me my set of works. The pain in my body was growing worse. My last fix had been seven o'clock the previous evening. By now, the muscles in my legs and arms had tightened. My whole body was tense. The first stages of stomach cramps were coming on. My nose was running—my head aching.

"I've got a bag of stuff in the cabinet in the bathroom," I continued my instructions to Ricky, using him as my nurse.

Like a good little errand boy, he had gathered up my instruments of death, including the little white bag of magic that was soon to take away all pain, sorrow, and suffering. In four to five seconds the snow-like powder was oozing through my veins. (Sometimes I could cook the dope, prepare the needle and syringe, and drill my vein in thirty seconds flat.)

Just as I was expecting to enjoy the "high," I suddenly slumped over, rolling off the side of the bed onto the floor. The drug was too strong. I had OD'd (taken an overdose of drugs). The power of the heroin rushed to my heart too fast, knocking me unconscious. It happened so quickly I didn't have time to remove the needle. When Ricky found me ten minutes later, my whole arm was bloody. My body had turned purple; my lips were stiff and cold.

Mom knew of my drug habit but had never seen anything like this. As she bent over my body—thinking I was dying or dead, she slapped my face, shaking my body, calling my name and praying, "Oh God, Oh God, please don't let him die." My arm moved slightly. Then in a few seconds (what must have seemed like an eternity to her) my eyes popped open as I slowly regained consciousness. The overdose had not been fatal. It very well could have been had the drug been just a small percentage stronger.

Mom and Ricky helped me back up on the bed. I pulled the needle out of my arm. Mom, still crying while catching her breath, was relieved to know her son, even if an addict, was still alive; put my face in her bosom.

With tears in her eyes she said, "Victor, my son, what are you doing to yourself? I thought we lost you. Don't you see what you're doing to yourself and to your mother? You're killing me, son."

Gently she laid my head down on the pillow. I looked up in my foggy semiconscious state—aware that once again my life had been on the abyss of death and hell—and tried to communicate my sorrow to her.

"I'm all right now, Mom. Please let me rest for a while," I said, wanting to be alone. She pulled the covers over me, patting my face with her hand, and walked quietly out of the room. At the door, she stood deeply sobbing and looked at me lying on the bed.

Alone—there was nothing for me to do but try to forget. A dope addict's life is made up of trying to forget.

Sure, the "high" is great. I would only be lying if I said it wasn't. It is a thrill, a kick, and a booster shot. But best of all, it kills pain.

And I don't mean just physical pain. It kills mental pain. It numbs the memory tank in the brain. Like magic, it curls your bad thoughts up into a little ball and hides them in the corner of your head. You feel good because your mind doesn't tell you how terrible things really are—how you have failed your parents; how you have failed yourself.

The problem is that as soon as the chemical fixer-upper wears off, that little ball of curled-up-bad-thoughts comes screaming back to life—and hits you like an electrical shock. If it's six or eight hours between heroin shots, then the body and bloodstream also react. "Feed me, baby" your body screams in emphatic terms. And you had better feed it or every muscle starts talking to you, sending frantic messages of pain and desperation to the brain. If you refuse to listen to its call for help, your body punishes you with unforgettable pain. The result is double trouble—a body that cannot function normally unless its bloodstream is constantly polluted with a poisonous drug and a mind and head that wants relief from agonizing thoughts. The only solution is to answer the call with the cure—snow ... dynamite ... junk.

That morning as I lay on the bed I tried to forget. I could not. It seemed as if my whole life came parading across my mind—like watching an "X" rated movie.

It started when I was seven. My parents lived in Puerto Rico but decided to go to New York. Like many others from our island and around the world, they thought they were going to the Promised Land. We were not really poor, but relatives and friends convinced Mom and Dad that New York offered so much more than we had. Dad went ahead of the rest of the family and said he would send for us as soon as possible. Though I was small I will never forget how excited we all were. Anxiously we waited for the word from Dad that we were to come.

It was a dream soon to become reality. My father had spoken about the better education his children would get, the greater job opportunities, and a bigger chance at life for us all. It was not that conditions were so terrible on the beautiful island of Puerto Rico. Our home was unbroken. We were a close family. Dad was a hard worker. We were getting by. Still, he was determined to explore this new land—and give us even a better life than what we had.

The experience of leaving our Caribbean island is stamped indelibly on my mind. The sun was shining as powerfully as it usually did—the air was so clean and rich. We all cried as we left our little country—our relatives, our friends, and our home.

Landing in New York, we were very anxious to meet my father. It had been six long months since we had seen him. I remember Father remarking about me, "You're so big, my little Victor. I can hardly recognize you." He picked me up and squeezed me tight. After greeting other relatives who were already settled in New York, we were off to our new home.

How different this new land was. Even I as a small lad could readily see the contrast. The sky was dark, the air cold, the buildings tall, and the cars seemed to run into each other. We didn't know what kind of neighborhood we were going to be living in, but as the car wound its way from the airport toward Brooklyn, the unpleasant picture unfolded before us little by little.

It wasn't until the next morning that we knew what our new place was really like. We had come to live in one of the roughest, dirtiest, and meanest neighborhoods in Brooklyn—the ghettos of Brownsville. It was the only housing my father could find. It had taken six months to secure it. Later I wished he never had.

"We'll move as soon as we can," Dad promised when he saw our disappointment. The apartment had no heating system; we had to use an old gas range in the kitchen to warm the entire place, which never quite worked. The walls and ceiling were crumbling, the paint peeling. We had no refrigerator. In the winter we used the window sills as our only means of refrigeration. But at least we had lots of company. Cockroaches, rats, and mice were our constant companions. They were everywhere—on the table when we ate, on the floor when we played, even on the bed when we slept.

We had arrived in the winter and on the third day of our arrival, it snowed. Ricky looked out the window, saw the falling flakes and yelled, "The moon is falling. Look, the moon is falling out of the sky in little bits!" We had never seen snow. My brother and I ran down the stairs as fast as we could onto the street. We wanted to feel the snow on our hands and faces—we even ate it. This was an entirely new experience, and a beautiful one—especially since the white powder was like a blanket, covering the ugliness and filth of the streets.

But soon the snow and dirt mixed together—it became an ugly mess. Winter was one of the four seasons we had come to wish they would have abolished. But the roughest time was the summer. The temperature would hit 100 or more. All the windows would be open and the noise and smells of the streets seemed to fill every corner and crevice of our apartment. At night our bedroom seemed as if it was in the middle of the street. During the day the street activity was a combination of a Coney Island amusement park and the jungle.

The days fell into four cycles. The kids took over the morning hours. In the afternoon the younger teens played their games. The early evening belonged to the parents and adults who played dominoes, cards, and rolled dice. The hours from 10 p.m. to 5 a.m. belonged to the winos, the drunks, the addicts, prostitutes, and gangs. There were nights you just wanted to go out of your mind. Even an insane asylum would have been better.

Because of the heat, the garbage smelled ten times worse. If the windows were closed it was suffocating. Then the rats and roaches completely took over. In the middle of the night, police cars rushed up and down the streets. A woman's screams pierced the night as she was mugged. Gunshots were common.

On one of those hot, humid nights, about two o'clock in the morning, our family was awakened by a blood-curdling shriek. I heard Mother shake Dad, "I think the sound came from the Rivera apartment upstairs."

"Get up, Manuel. Get up and go see," Mom said. Dad quickly slipped on his trousers, unbolted the door and made his way up the dimly lit stairs. Mom went to the door to watch.

The Rivera door was locked. I heard Dad yell, "Mrs. Rivera. What happened? Let me inside. It's Mr. Torres. Let me in."

The door opened to a screaming mother who was beside herself, "My baby, it's my baby! Oh, my God, my poor little child! The face ... look at the face ... help ... please do something. A rat bit my baby's face." My father rushed in to find the nine-month-old Rivera baby girl bleeding from bites on the cheek and forehead. A rat had climbed right into the crib.

Dad washed out the wounds and bandaged them. Mom went up and comforted a terrified Mrs. Rivera.

A few months later a rat bit a boy's leg in another family in our building. All of this had its effect upon my nine-year-old mind and emotions. Neither did it escape my little brother and baby sister. We all lived in constant fear. My father worked in a factory—at night. He would leave the apartment in the afternoon and not get home until two o'clock in the morning. As I remember it, we usually waited up for him. We were very afraid for ourselves and were gripped with fear that something might happen to him on his way home. So, we waited.

The entire family lived in tension every night waiting for Dad to come home. Every night was another crisis—thinking about him riding the subway, walking the dark and dangerous streets. In the summer we watched from the window to see him coming down the street. If we were in bed we listened for his whistle. He always whistled coming up the stairs, unless he was in trouble. Gang members or thieves would often hide in the building waiting to mug somebody. We knew Dad wasn't safe until he was not only inside our building, but safely inside the apartment and had locked and bolted the door. Then off to sleep we would go—relieved for another night.

I often asked my father, "When are we going to get out of this hole?"

He'd look at me with sadness in his eyes. All he could say was, "Someday we will have a better place to live... someday."

In the meantime out of necessity, we adjusted the best we could to life in the asphalt jungle. I wasn't doing a very good job of it. Sometimes my brother Ricky, sister Elizabeth, and I cried ourselves to sleep. The conditions affected us all in different ways, but we were powerless to do anything about it.

When we first moved into the neighborhood, my parents went to church. In Puerto Rico, we attended the Disciples of Christ Church. They took us every Sunday and almost every time there was a service. But after about a year in New York, they stopped going. Why—I don't exactly know. Perhaps because of my father's job. He was too busy trying to survive to have time for anything else. As I look back now perhaps if we had continued to go to church regularly, drugs might never have been a part of my life.

My father was making $45 a week. It wasn't enough, so Mother went to work also. Dad left for his job at 3 o'clock in the afternoon, and Mom didn't get home until six. The three of us children were left alone for those hours, which I spent mostly on the streets. I paid a price to do so. Life on the streets was a contest—every day. I constantly had to prove myself. Groups and cliques formed, and to break into one—to be "in"—it was necessary to prove yourself; to gain attention, respect, identity, and friends. If you were big enough or loud enough, you could fake it. I couldn't.

I was small—and skinny. Big talk didn't do me any good. I had to fight. It didn't seem to matter if I won or lost (although it mattered to my body), but as far as the crowd was concerned as long as you proved you had guts, it was enough. The idea was never to back down. Many days I came home having proven my courage at the price of a bloody nose or a bruised, aching body.

At the age of twelve, I decided to make some money by going into the shoe-shine business. A few weeks after starting and while working in front of our building a neighborhood boy of about fifteen approached me.

"What's your name?" he asked wise-guy fashion. "Victor," I answered as I fixed my shoe-shine kit. "You tough?" he quickly asked.

"Can be," I said without looking up. Before I knew what was happening he kicked me to the ground and was on top of me punching away at my body.

"Let's just see how tough you are, you little shoe-shine punk!" I reacted quickly to defend myself. I was small but quick. In a flash I had him turned over and pounded a fist into his face. He jumped off the sidewalk into the gutter. We both stood in a half crouch ready to move at each other like two opposing jungle animals. He spotted a pipe, grabbed it and lunged at my head. I managed to get my hand in the way of the swinging weapon. It hit my arm instead of my head. The pipe broke loose from the impact and fell to the street.

"You were lucky," he said, walking away leaving me clutching my arm in agony. "Next time it might be your head."

My arm was broken from that episode, but the ache inside was worse. I'd get up in the morning dreading to face another day. "What is going to happen to me today?" I would ask myself. I walked the streets with eyes wide open ready to defend myself. I always looked over my shoulder because there was no safety, even for a moment. I was jumped in the gutter so many times, I expected trouble to erupt at any time. I felt like a wanted criminal whose only crime was that he lived on the block.

On another occasion, I was shining some black boots for my first customer of the morning. I told the man to lean back on a big dark blue Pontiac nearby. I was just putting the finishing touches on the spit-shine when I heard someone running toward us hollering, "You son of a bitch!

What you doin'? Who gave you permission to use my car as a chair? Get out of here!"

"Look, I didn't mean anything by it, mister. We ain't hurtin' your car." I pleaded for his understanding.

He was angry—mean angry. I had seen his kind before. Before I could grab the shoe-shine box, he grabbed my hair. "You dirty little Spic. Bug off! This ain't your neighborhood anyway. Get over to the garbage hole where you belong."

He kicked me, then grabbed me by the shirt and threw me down on the street. I lay motionless for a moment, not moving an inch but looking up with fear and defiance.

"Did you hear what I said?" he roared, coming at me again.

As he did I rattled off some curse words in Spanish. That was a mistake. It always bothered white men who didn't understand the Spanish language, and understood Spanish-speaking people even less. In fact, they hated us more when we spoke a few unkind words in our native tongue. Spanish speaking people delighted doing this to the non-Spanish speaking people. It was one thing we possessed that they did not. It was a way of retaining our own identity.

The Pontiac owner was now furious. He kicked at me again, causing me to roll out into the street where I was almost hit by a passing car. Now in panic, I reached into my pocket for a knife. Since the broken arm episode, I had decided to carry some protection. The knife was a daily companion. I opened it quickly and as he came around to swing at me I stabbed him in the side, under the left armpit.

It took him a few seconds to discover what happened. Then he screamed, "I've been stabbed! I've been stabbed! This dirty Spic stuck a blade in me! Somebody call the cops!"

A crowd gathered. I backed off and quietly crouched down beside his car, on the street side. He staggered over in front of a candy store, holding his side. Blood was all over his shirt. It had all happened so fast that it didn't really dawn on me the damage I had done until I saw all the blood. Then I knew I was in trouble. Fear and panic gripped me so I ran. Our house was just around the corner.

I beat my little twelve-year-old feet on the pavement as fast as my skinny legs could carry them. Running up the stairs to our apartment, I forgot the knife was in my hand. Realizing I still had it and seeing the blood on my hand, I ditched the knife under the stairway leading to the basement. Then I dashed up the stairs two and three at a time.

I ran into the apartment shaking, feeling the coldness of blood running down on my hand.

Mom was in the kitchen. "Victor. What's the matter with you? What happened?" She could see the state of fright I was in.

"I just stabbed a man. He was trying to kill me. I had to do it. I had to defend myself." I went on to tell her how bad it was, making it sound like it was almost death for me unless I defended myself. I needed Mom on my side.

"Did anyone see you do it?"

"Yeah, a whole bunch of people watched."

"Then the police will be looking for you. What will I do if they come? I wish your father was here."

"I gotta hide, Mom," I suggested.

"All right, get under the bed. I'll tell them I don't know where you are," she said, pushing me out of the kitchen into the bedroom. "But I can't speak English," she remembered, wondering how she would communicate with the police.

I shook with fear as I lay under the bed sobbing quietly. I knew it would only be a matter of time till the cops came. People on the street who saw me do it knew where I lived.

After what seemed like hours but was only about twenty minutes, there was banging on the door. My body jumped when I heard the loud fist bang on the door.

Two policemen came bursting in after Mom unlocked the door. Mom told them in Spanish no one was home. They ignored her and started looking around. I had done a poor job of hiding—a shoe was showing from under the bed. "OK, fella, come with us," the officer said as he pulled me out from under the bed. "Tell your mother to come along to the precinct."

At the Seventy-Third Police Station, after a lot of discussion and deliberation, they arrested me, but let me go home and said I would be notified when to go to family court for the outcome. Weeks later I was placed on probation for an indefinite period. I was fortunate they didn't send me to reform school.

This became a turning point in my young life. In spite of the warnings, pleadings, lectures, and beatings from Mom and Dad, I was on a downhill journey. Hate slowly formed in my mind and heart. Life disillusioned me. Why did these things have to happen to me? Why did I have to live in such miserable surroundings? Like wet soft cement, my heart began to set and harden. Deep down I didn't want it that way, but too many ugly things were happening to prevent it. I did want to please Mom and Dad and live a halfway decent life. I had ambitions and goals, but the fifteen-year-old, who banged my head in and broke my arm, and the big guys that kicked me, called me dirty names for being different and a foreigner, kept interrupting those ambitions. My castles crumbled.

Survival was my role. The evil streets were conditioning my attitudes and behavior patterns—I was becoming a product and a son, of those evil streets.

# 2

# THE "GIG" SCHOOL

There was no escape there either. At first, I tried to learn.

My father had a small business in Puerto Rico before we moved and I thought about following in his footsteps one day. I wanted to make it good and be a "somebody" in life. But school was no launching pad for me and it became the dead end.

School for a fourteen-year-old teenager in a Brooklyn Junior High was literally a "blackboard jungle." Every day I made new friends—and enemies. What was started in school—arguments, threats, name-calling—was finished outside. I had to fight my way into school, and often fight my way out. If the battle couldn't wait it took place in the hallways, bathroom, or even the classroom. There were no police on patrol in the schools, so we just about controlled the place. There were very few school days when something didn't break loose. Some days I dreaded going to school. I felt that instead of school, I was walking into a living hell, and I often wondered if I would survive.

One day coming out of school I recognized a guy by the name of Big Ray approaching me. I braced myself because we had never met and he was one of the biggest guys around the neighborhood. He was known for his meanness and toughness and was appropriately called, "Big Ray."

Coming along aside me he tapped the side of my leg, "Want to go to a party?"

"Yeah, man. I'm game," I answered, trying to be excited yet a little suspicious as to why he would walk up to me and make such an invitation.

I guess he recognized my guarded enthusiasm and said, "Listen, baby, I been watching you and you're pretty bad. I want you to meet some of the guys from the neighborhood. Let's see if the chicks dig you. If they do, you're in. Some of the dudes you know will be there too." He explained the whole setup as we continued walking down the street. The more he talked the bigger I felt.

After he gave me the address to go to that evening I said, "You can count on me, man. I'll see you at eight."

As I turned into my building Big Ray said, "You're going to have a blast, man."

I couldn't wait. This was the first gang meeting I had ever been invited to. It was my "coming out" party. My entrance into the world and manhood—as it was viewed on my block. To be invited to the local neighborhood party, by the biggest and most popular dude, was like being told, "You're in."

"Don't blow it, Victor," I said to myself, walking toward Christopher Avenue and the site of the party. I found the old broken-down building Big Ray described. It was a condemned place where the gang had helped themselves to the basement for a meeting place. I walked carefully down the dark corridor leading to a door I saw at the back of the basement. I was careful not to get my suit dirty from the walls, especially after spending over an hour to get dressed up. I lied to Mom and told her I was going to a school dance. It was the first time she had seen me take so much time to look nice.

I reached the door with the words "Roman Lords" handwritten in big letters over the door. I heard music inside. A big lump came into my stomach as I knocked on the door.

Inside I saw a few friends. "Hi, Eddie, how you doing," I half whispered. It was good to see a familiar face. Still, I felt strange. I took a seat and looked around. The lights were dim. About twenty guys and girls were packed into the small room with soft music playing from a cheap record player in the corner. Some danced, tightly, in the middle of the floor. A few sat huddled close together drinking beer and wine. "Have a taste man," a voice, whose face I couldn't identify in the shadows, said.

"Thanks," I said taking a small gulp. I handed the bottle back and then caught a whiff of a peculiar odor. I kept sniffing while trying not to look as if I didn't know what was happening. "Smells like oregano," I said to myself. "It must be to sweeten the air." I heard a couple of the guys make funny noises with their mouths. They were smoking cigarettes. Soon the place was filled with smoke and the strange smelling sweet odor. A feeling of uneasiness hit me in the pit of my stomach. I knew something different was going on, something I had never experienced before. I sensed that what was going to happen was dangerous—and I couldn't wait to find out.

Fifteen minutes passed without any action coming my way. I tried to appear hip to the whole scene, but I was not doing a very good job. Finally, Little Joe approached me and said, "What'a you doin' here?"

"Big Ray invited me," I answered proudly. He shook his head approvingly.

"Wanna taste somethin' that will really flip you out? Come on, I'll turn you on," he said with a sheepish grin.

"What you got?" I asked, trying not to appear too anxious.

"Grass, man. You never seen any grass like this," he answered. Little Joe took out a cigarette about one and a half inches in length. The ends were curled and twisted together in homemade fashion. After lighting it, he showed me how to burn it so the smoke would stay in the lungs as long as possible.

"That's the way you get high," he explained.

I carefully followed his detailed instructions and took a deep drag. Nothing happened. I took another drag, holding in the smoke as long as I could stand it; coughing on and off. Slowly I felt the drug's effect. My head started getting light. I felt dizzy. I sat down in the corner and puffed away. My head felt pounds lighter, as though it wasn't there.

Later I wanted to dance. From one chick to the next I danced. As the evening wore on, I danced and danced and talked and talked. I thought I was the best dancer on the floor. But in reality, I could hardly move my feet. Grass was a real turn-on, just like Little Joe promised. I was not disappointed. It turned me into something I was not. I could talk to the girls, and I felt free and loose. I could be like I always wanted to be with a group; relaxed, uninhibited, cool, hip, and free of my inferiority complex. I actually thought I was the best dancer in the whole party, and the happiest person. For about four hours I was in a new world. In spite of the dirty, dingy basement in an abandoned, broken-down apartment house in one of the worst neighborhoods in New York City, everything was beautiful, at least in my head. I was on a trip—a mind trip. For those few precious hours that other world of reality was off somewhere in the distance. It was as if a bubble was created around me shutting off the evil, the misery, the hate, and the confusion of Powell Street and my neighborhood.

# 3

# THE ROMAN LORDS

A few days after the party, I asked one of the guys, "Where can I get some grass?"

Big Ray "is the connection," I was told. "He's the gardener," they said as they laughed at the description.

"Grows real nice grass that Ray does," was another party goer's comment. They advertised it well.

When I found Big Ray he was glad to offer me a few joints. "Only fifty cents to my friends," he said.

After purchasing two joints from him, he asked me, "Victor, how would you like to join the gang?"

Big Ray served a dual role on the block. He was the friendly neighborhood pusher as well as an active member of a local street gang called The Roman Lords. What I hadn't known was that he invited me to the party so the gang could look me over to see if I was a good prospect to join them. Evidently, I must have done something right, or Big Ray was just pleased to have another customer. At any rate, he officially invited me to join.

But joining a street gang is not like joining a social club or a political organization. Being asked to join is not the same as acceptance. I had to pass initiation.

I told Big Ray, "Anytime you're ready to test me, I'll be ready to prove myself." I sounded tough, but I didn't even know the initiation procedure.

I was told to report the same night to a park called Betsy Head, about six blocks from my house.

At approximately nine o'clock that evening, I walked slowly toward the park, butterflies fluttering in my stomach. I said to myself, "What am I getting into now?" In a way, I wished I wasn't going to join the gang, but in another way was excited. It was a proud moment in my life when I was invited to the party and now being asked to prove myself for gang initiation was the icing on the cake. I was finally making it with the "big" guys on the block. I was going to belong. It was a good feeling to be wanted. Being "one of the guys" is what I had lived for since the day I arrived in Brownsville and started hanging out with the older guys.

Even if I didn't want to join the gang, I really had no choice. I needed their protection. I couldn't afford to go it alone anymore and face the dangers of the street life. The Roman Lords offered me a chance for security—and identity. When I walked into Betsy Head it was like walking into the insurance office. "You're in good hands with the Roman Lords," I was assured by their agents.

Arriving at the park I stopped daydreaming, realizing I wasn't in the gang yet. About a hundred guys and gals were standing around. At the sight of them, a sense of fear shot through me.

"Here comes the next victim!" someone yelled, not helping the situation.

"We'll see if he's a punk soon enough," I heard from another voice whose face I couldn't see in the dark.

Others yelled, "Knock the crap out of these new dudes!" "Kick 'em in the face."

"Spill their guts!"

I, along with a few other guys scheduled for the initiation, was led to the middle of the crowd. I wanted to run. But, now it was impossible.

"All right, knock it off," someone said as he stood on a park bench. His name was Beebop. He was about five feet, ten inches tall, a little on the thin side, but strong. He had to be the president. I heard that he had "heart."

It meant he was not afraid of blood. He never backed down. A lot of gang members did. He was a natural leader and spoke with a leader's authority. He was bad and had a look on his face that was frightening. The members looked up to him.

I listened as Beebop gave out plans for a future rumble. I was impressed with how well they were organized.

The organizational structure of a gang and the supporting forces included: president, vice-president, sergeant-of-arms, war counselor, active fighting members, inactive members, phonies, straights, debs, and dolls.

The inactive members were usually too chicken to fight, but were forced to join to ensure a show of a large force of strength to another gang if there was a really big rumble. Even if they never fought, their presence sometimes served a purpose.

The straights were the good kids who attended school and whose parents kept them home most of the time and they kept out of trouble. These included churchgoing youth.

The phonies were made up of some active gang members, but mostly inactive guys who would make like they were a part of the gang but never actually got into the action.

During a rumble, they would go with the rest of the gang to fight but then hide under parked cars, in hallways or basements. When the rumble was all over they would come back saying, "We sure messed them up, didn't we?" Some would rub dirt on themselves, mark up their clothes, and even try to get blood on themselves to make it look good. If we ever caught one of our guys being phony, we would beat him to a pulp.

After Beebop finished laying out the plans, he yelled, "All right, all you cats goin' to be proved, step forward." There were three of us.

"Here's what you have to do. Either you run the gauntlet and we throw punches into your gut or you fight one of the regular members of my choosing."

"Some choice," I thought to myself. I decided to fight. The idea was not necessarily to win or lose but to beat each other unmercifully. You had to make a good showing and prove you could take a tough beating. Everyone watched closely to see if you panicked, flinched, or backed down. They were testing me to see if I could hang, if I could endure a gang street fight. It was more of a "gut test" than a fight.

Beebop chose my opponent. He was one of the toughest members of The Roman Lords—as I was to find out later. I am glad I didn't know that when we started or he might have psyched me out.

The fight was a standoff. We threw fists at first, both landing a few good body punches and a couple solid hits on the face. Then we swung wild and ended up wrestling each other to the ground. Then we wrestled and punched until we both almost collapsed, but we didn't dare quit. Finally, Beebop interrupted, "Cool it, cool it. That's enough. Put it there, Victor. You're in, man. You showed yourself." We slapped hands.

A few other gang members shook my hand. I stood with them watching the next guy go through his initiation. It was a proud moment standing with the gang, knowing I was one of them. The excitement was dulled by my aching body and head. But I felt ten feet tall on the inside.

There wasn't time to enjoy my gang entry. Beebop called us together after initiations were over.

He announced, "Some of you know we're goin' after the Liberty Boys. They've been talking real big about comin' to get us. We'll get the jump on 'em. I don't like what they did to Nina the other day. That dude Archie got nasty with her."

Beebop went on about some other so-called rumors of what the Liberty Boys said and did. I was to learn later that the "reasons why we got to bust their heads in," were partly true but mostly made up. It was all a part of the gang leader's role to "psyche" up his members. We had many such "psyche sessions" during the course of my gang activity. The president's lecture was all some guys needed to build up their anger and emotions to get ready to rumble. Others needed wine, whiskey, beer or pot to boost them up and give them courage. For some, it was courage they did not possess.

The next day we met at a prescribed time. Again, Beebop took a short time to get us ready emotionally. He took up where he left off the night before, telling how they were after our women. He was interrupted, "Hey Beebop. Know what one of the Liberty Boys called my mom? I won't even repeat it. I'm gonna burn that son-of-a-bitch if I get my hands on 'im."

"Put a bullet in him," someone called out.

Still, another yelled, "Kick his head in."

It was time to go. The president realized we had reached the peak of emotion and anger.

He gave last minute instructions about the rumble. It was to be a surprise attack on the Liberty Boys' hangout at the corner of Liberty Avenue and Pennsylvania Avenue.

"I want you to leave here walking in groups of six, three in the front and three about two feet behind. No one breathe a word. We gotta play this cool like nothing is gonna happen. Like we're gonna go play pool or somethin'. And we got to spread out so we don't look like an army marchin' off to war—even though that's exactly what we're gonna be doin'. And you dudes better listen to me when I give the signal and make war. You hear me," Beebop said authoritatively.

We all affirmed his leadership as we made our way to the target area, everyone with his custom-made jacket. "The Roman Lords" stood out boldly in big red letters on the black jackets.

We all had weapons. The night before there had been a few tense moments among us as we decided on the type of weapons we would use.

"What weapons?" one of the guys asked.

"Pipes, bats, knuckles, antennas, and blades," Beebop ran down the list of our usual arsenal.

"What about guns?'

'Yeah man, let's really lay it on 'em."

Beebop hesitated. We waited for his answer. Guns were the real symbol of the gang. Some felt you were not a man and had no real guts unless you were not afraid to use a gun. Other guys preferred pipes, bats, or knuckles. Some used only a blade. They were the ones who wanted to see blood. Some got their kicks just out of slashing or stabbing. I saw guys almost go wild with joy when they bled another rival gang member.

"All right," Beebop broke the silence. "If any of you want to use guns go ahead. Just make sure you shoot straight. You will look stupid lying on the street from your own bullet."

He had to agree to guns or it might appear he was afraid of them. He couldn't afford the least bit show of weakness or fear. Beebop was a blade man himself.

In my pack of guys, I noticed the choice of weapons. Sammy had a pipe; Billy, brass knuckles; and Willie had something I had never seen before. It was a chain about three feet long. On the end were fishhooks. Tied onto the fishhooks were lead weights.

"Where you goin', Willie? Fishing," I asked with a nervous laugh.

"Yeah, that's just what I'm planning to do—fishing.' I'm fishing for flesh, man-flesh. I'm going to get me a hunk of one of those Liberty Boys. I want to rip their face wide open."

We continued walking the ten blocks or so to the combat area located on the edge of their turf. About two blocks from that point we slowed down. Our walk became more deliberate—sneaky like. I had a funny feeling in my stomach and I felt my muscles tighten. In my first rumble, there were a lot of things to consider. I had to protect myself from getting beat up. Most of all I had to prove to the other guys and myself that I had courage and could kill a rival gang member. I wondered, could I beat and kill someone if necessary?

A block away we spotted their hangout. It was a pool room and combination social club.

Not only did we have to make sure the Liberty Boys did not spot us; there were the cops to watch out for as well. It was summer so they were thick in the neighborhood. Sometimes they could sense trouble and head off a rumble. Their job was to cut it off by arresting members of the gang or flood the rumble area with squad cars. Rumbles could turn into complete neighborhood riots with older gang graduates and even adults getting into the action. We wanted a rumble, not a riot.

Our group of guys waited in the doorway of an apartment house. We could see some of the Liberty Boys hanging around inside and outside the pool room. We stood and patiently waited for Beebop to give the word, like animals ready to attack their prey.

Then the word came loud and clear through the air, "Burn 'em! Burn 'em!" Roman Lords poured out into the street from every direction. Our voices filled the air.

"Down with the Liberty Boys!" "Kill 'em! Kill 'em!"

We converged on the corner. I could hear shots. We caught them completely unaware. They had virtually no defense weapons, except those who carried pocketknives. The secret of a gang victory is surprise. They were trapped.

I had a pipe. As I moved into the action a Liberty Boy was about to put a knife into Billy. I hit him on the back, spun him around and kicked the knife out of his hand. I swung the pipe from back to front over my head. He moved back.

Another guy came toward me. I swung the pipe at him but he ducked under it. I had to use my fist to defend myself and landed a punch on his mouth. The force of the punch as he came running at me created a terrible impact—terrible for him. His lip bled profusely and I broke one of his teeth. That resulted in tearing the flesh in my hand.

I backed off from the scene and saw many getting hurt. In the heat of the battle the real man—or boy—came out. Some couldn't take it. There were cries of "Oh, my God ... I've been hurt." The most pitiful cases were the guys who cried, "Mama, Mama," who were in their first rumble. It is easy to be a tough gang member when wearing the jacket, planning the rumble, and hanging out on the street corner. It's another story in the middle of a war.

Most of us were laughing and digging the scene. In the excitement, we hollered and screamed as we unleashed our anger.

A few of the Liberty Boys made the mistake of going inside their clubhouse. We chased after them.

Beebop gave the order, "Drag 'em out." Three of us grabbed one of them, shoving him out the door. He tried to escape but Sammy tackled him. We stomped our feet on him, kicking his face, ribs, and back. He moaned quietly in pain.

We were wild now. I had become like a mad dog. It was like we were high under the influence of some strange drug—in a spirit of violence. The action was at the point where we lost our heads and did just what our uncontrolled emotions dictated us to do.

Glass shattered and I looked up in time to see a Liberty Boy coming through the glass window of the clubhouse. To add insult to injury, Willie, the fishhook man, and Sundown ripped off his clothes leaving him lying naked in the gutter.

It all ended as suddenly as it began. "Cops … here comes the Cops; get out of here" somebody yelled. Then the big run followed. Down the streets we scrambled, some going through the backyards to keep out of sight, others going into basement passageways. There was strategy even when splitting from a rumble. If we bunched up the cops could round us up. If we scattered it was impossible for them to find us. For about thirty minutes we lay low— then went home, to a secret hideout, or to a girlfriend's house. I knew of one guy who even went to church. For two or three hours we kept out of sight, then came together to celebrate victory. Out came the cans of beer, whiskey, and pot. The guys who got hurt drank the most, trying to dull the pain.

We really didn't know the damage the rumble caused until the next day when the papers carried part of the story of what happened. Even if it didn't make the papers (it was considered a good rumble if it did), the rumors spread fast and furious. Our stories were always prefabricated, but we had done enough damage to the Liberty Boys so that it was not necessary to add to what we had done.

The day after the gang war we all felt good—and big. We had proved our manhood. What we didn't have in character or intelligence, at least we felt we made up for in courage and heart. We might not be "somebody" at home, in school, or in the eyes of most people in the neighborhood. But we were "somebody" in the eyes of our fellow gang members—and especially the eyes of Liberty Boys.

Being "somebody" didn't last long. I found it to be a very temporary state. It usually lasted until the rival gang retaliated and tried to re-establish its own identity and reputation. But for the moment we were king of the neighborhood. Each of us had a little hill on that mountain of his very own. For the next few days, we bragged, walked with heads held high and proud, and flaunted our victory. To me, it was a great feeling.

Our victory also had a psychological effect on the other gangs bordering us. All over Brooklyn, we fought the Frenchmen, the Chester Avenue Boys, the Mau Maus from Fort Greene, the Flattops, Viceroys, and the Hell Burners. When they heard of our wipe-out of the Liberty Boys, it had an effect on their attitude toward us when we did go against them. They thought twice about taking the first step to come at us. We even heard that the police assigned extra men to patrol our area. We really ate that up. We were living up to our ancient namesakes—The Roman Lords.

When we weren't rumbling we got to know and see the policemen in a different light. Our favorite policeman was nicknamed "Mousie." Whenever he came into our neighborhood with another policeman, especially a new one, he got tough with us and pushed around a few guys. We knew he was showing off, because when he was alone we could sense his fear. So we gave him the name "Mousie the Cop."

Once in the local park, Mousie approached us. Sometimes he would just stop and chat.

"Hey, look who's comin'," one of the guys said, calling our attention to our favorite man in blue. One of the guys screamed out, "Mousie!"

He hated the name we had tagged on him. Hearing it his face flushed and he stiffened up.

"Hey, Mousie," went out the second call. The latter triggered his anger and he made a beeline straight for us. "Listen you punks, I'll run you in, the whole bunch!"

"Oh yeah, with whose help?" he was asked.

The group of us stood as one and took a step toward him. He stopped. Then as if it had been planned, Beebop jumped Mousie, grabbing his neck while the rest of us pulled him to the ground.

"Take him to the bathroom," someone suggested, referring to the restrooms located within the park premises. We took him to the men's room and removed his gun and badge.

"Strip him. Let's strip him," another guy suggested.

We were wild with excitement and mischief. In minutes we had him stripped completely naked.

"Wow! Look at that. He sure is pretty."

We laughed in triumph, taunting and whistling.

We left the park, leaving Mousie with no gun, no clothes, and no place to go unless he dared walk the streets in the nude.

We decided to call the station house and inform the local precinct that a naked cop was on the loose in the park.

We laughed for days about naked Mousie, but we also knew we would be on his wanted list, as well as the entire local force. One way or the other, they would try to make The Roman Lords sorry for what they had done.

# 4

# STAY DOWN IN THE GUTTER

I worked my way up the gang totem pole. From a new arrival on Powell Street as a skinny little kid from Puerto Rico, I graduated to a pot head in the neighborhood "gigs." Then finally the big step to the gang. There I was respected. I felt wanted—and needed. My reputation as a "jitter-bugger" was good. The guys considered me to have some brains as well. They often sought my advice on matters. When they didn't and I put in my two cents and they listened.

The reward of brawn and brains ended in a promotion in the gang to Sergeant-of-Arms. I was the weapon man.

I made them, hid them, and often selected the ones we would use. The position made me third man from the top.

Oddly enough, I got my training for Sergeant-of-Arms through my membership in the local Brooklyn Boys Club. It was there I learned to work with wood and woodcutting machines.

When I joined the gang I simply applied my abilities to making zip guns. I made sure I went to all the club meetings so I could cut out another wood form for a gun, sneaking it out to our gang hideout where I put the finishing touches on it.

When I wasn't making guns, going off and on to school, or smoking marijuana, I played pool at our favorite hang out.

One day after shooting a few games, I was standing outside when a kid from the block rode up on his bike.

"Hey, let me show you a few tricks," I said, not waiting to ask for the use of the bike but just taking it and riding off down the street. Up and down I went, zigzagging, riding with no hands, doing figure eights. Then getting real smart I began riding backward.

"Look guys. I could join the circus." I called their attention to my ability to ride backward.

"Watch it, Victor!" someone yelled as I picked up speed weaving back and forth down the street.

"There's a car, Victor! Look out for the car!" I was too busy showing off to hear.

A big Cadillac came slowly around the corner. Zigzagging my way along, I accidentally bumped into his fender. The impact knocked me off the bike, rolling me into the gutter.

The driver slammed on his brakes and rushed to my side. Others came quickly.

"You, all right? You hurt, Victor?" they asked.

I was stunned a little but wasn't injured. My pride was wounded more so than my body. I was getting up off the ground brushing off the dirt when suddenly a man ran over to me. He grabbed me and in one quick motion pushed me back down on the street. As he did so he whispered in my ear, "Listen, man, I saw what happened. Stay down right where you are. Don't move an inch. Make believe you broke something. Don't get up. Don't be a fool. You just been hit by a car—that's serious."

I was bewildered for a moment. I looked up from my prone position and recognized the Jewish man from the corner cleaners.

I got his message loud and clear. In mechanical style fashion the gears started clicking in my head. It dawned on me what he was up to. I started screaming, "Oh, my God, dear God, I'm hurt. I've been hit. Help! Somebody, please help me! I think I'm gonna die."

I made it sound good. The hardest thing was to keep from laughing.

The other guys got the message as well. Willie yelled at the driver, "Why didn't you watch where you were going?"

"You were like a madman behind that wheel," another piped in.

Then they all started getting into the act. "I bet he's even drunk."

"He was going about fifty miles an hour."

"He was trying to run you over, Victor I saw him."

The whole clique of guys hanging out on the corner got the message and played it to the hilt.

"I was only going fifteen miles an hour. I purposely slowed down 'cause I saw him out of control on the bike. He banged into me—what could I do?" The poor driver tried to defend himself against the trumped-up charges.

He was beside himself not knowing what to do. I guess he couldn't believe what was going on before his eyes. Then he got angry and yelled, "You're trying to frame me!"

Big Ray made his way through the crowd and addressed himself to the driver. "You better shut up, mister, before we make this a courtroom right here and now. We got ourselves a jury all ready to hear this case."

Turning to the crowd he said, "Isn't that right?"

"Yeah, we'll convict you right now. We may just decide to punish you right here by jumping you, man."

The cops then arrived. The Jewish man set me up on a chair and took me inside his store. While the crowd had been picking on the driver, he had gone off to call the police, an ambulance—and a lawyer.

Before the police could question me, he leaned over and said, "Just play along, fella. I got a plan. You're going to get a bundle of money out of this if you do just what I tell you."

"Oh my back officer, it's my back. I think it's broken," I moaned to the police when they asked how I felt. All the while complaining about a broken back I was sitting on a chair.

In all the confusion no one was smart enough to see the flaw in my act. At the hospital, I had to continue the drama. Examination papers were filled out on the accident and on my supposed injury. As the hospital attendant filled out the papers, every few minutes I let out a groan. Finally, the attendant said, "You can relax now. Cut the act."

"Did you put everything down? I'm not going to sign anything 'till you put down how I'm messed up," I insisted.

"Everything is in order," he assured me. As quickly as I turned on my performance, I turned it off.

A lawyer came to visit me while I was still in the emergency ward. He also took down all the details of my "accident." With an out-of-court settlement with the insurance company of the driver—I came out with $2,000 on the deal. The Jewish man, of course, got his cut, as well as the lawyer and who knows who else, perhaps the hospital aide. I didn't care. I had mine.

"You should have won an Oscar for that acting job," the guys joked about it after the settlement.

I had learned my first big lesson in the game of conning. The reward was an automobile. I decided to take the money and purchase a car. I was only fifteen at the time, but through a friend in the Roman Lords named Tony Baby Face, I was able to get the car. It came equipped with forged registration and plates. My one major problem was that I couldn't get a license. I did know how to drive the car, and once stopped by the police a ten-dollar bill slipped into the officer's hand was good enough to keep me from getting arrested. I had to remember never go anywhere without a ten-dollar bill in my pocket. I must have paid out approximately three hundred dollars in that fashion before I turned sixteen and could legalize my driving. So many of the cops knew my car, they automatically stopped me to pick up a little extra bread.

Not only was I popular with the police; I also gained instant popularity with the girls.

The car served another purpose. It took me and the guys and gals I always had with me when cruising around—into another world. Now we were able to get out of the slums and into the nicer neighborhoods. With wheels we were privileged to go places and see things other gang members and ghetto kids in their teens rarely had a chance to see. For us, going out of the neighborhood was like a trip to Florida or California. We broke out of the hell hole. The automobile gave us a mobility even my parents and many other ghetto adults did not have.

The most important function the car served, however, was that it gave me something other than the gang to depend on for excitement and kicks. For some members of the gang, the gang was everything. They had nothing else going for them. The president was like their father; the vice-president, like a mother; the other gang guys like brothers to them; and the girls were like sisters or their real girlfriends. Sometimes they would sleep at their own home, but other than that, "home" was the local street corner, the candy store, the pool room, or the gang hideout. Not many broke out of the gang syndrome. It was a daily merry-go-round and sometimes misery-go-round of a few thrills, a lot of cheap talk, cheap wine, cheap grass, and cheap sex. I was lucky—the car was my passport on rubber to the outside world. It became my four-wheel pad full of gang friends, a lot of chicks—and stolen goods.

I hadn't planned on becoming a thief. It just happened naturally like many other things seemed to just happen in that environment. Going out of Brownsville into the better sections of the city, I was able to see how the "haves" were getting along. I liked what I saw. I wanted what I saw. A friend suggested we pull some jobs. It all seemed so easy. We just loaded stuff we "ripped off," into the trunk and returned to Brownsville; nobody knew the difference. It was easier than I thought.

Our first rip-off was characterized by one of the guys as a "firecracker" of a job. Cruising along one night through an Italian section of Brooklyn, Freddie spotted an expensive looking apartment house. He suggested, "Let's park and try the basement of this place. They use the basement as storage areas. I bet we can find ourselves some nice things."

We parked and walked around a corner into an alleyway behind the apartment. It was just turning dark. Making our way through a passageway I bumped into an object, nearly stumbling to the ground. "Shit!" I yelled as I balanced myself by grabbing one of the other guys.

"You're sure a clumsy crook," Louis threw a wisecrack at me.

"Wow, look at this. Look what I ran into, boxes. They're sure heavy," I said. "Find a light."

Louis found a string attached to a light and pulled it. The light revealed a stack of about fifty boxes piled one on top of another next to the basement wall. I opened a box.

"It's dynamite. Can you beat that—we found ourselves some explosives!" Freddie exclaimed like a child opening a Christmas package.

"Dynamite, my ass," I said. "These are firecrackers. Man, there must be half a ton here. Every one of these boxes are loaded with 'em."

"Some cat must do a real business. These things are against the law in New York State," Freddie informed us. Then in his familiar self-righteous manner, he said,

"There's some dishonest dude living here. He ought to be ashamed of himself. I bet he's a Mafia guy."

"Shut up and quit your bullshit," I said, counting the boxes and doing some quick figuring in my head.

"There must be close to fifteen thousand dollars worth of fireworks here. This is a good haul. We'll make a bundle with this."

Freddie couldn't keep from viewing the whole thing philosophically. "Let's pull a Robin Hood and steal from the rich. Anyway, we'll be doing this neighborhood a favor by getting rid of this. Think of all the noise these cherry bombs would make here. Why don't we sell them over in our neighborhood—we're more used to noise."

I looked at Freddie, "Are you finished?" He nodded. "Let's pull the car closer to the alley and load up." While a couple guys stood watch, we loaded sixteen more boxes in the car. It took three trips to clear out the basement. We stored them in our gang hideout.

By midnight we had carefully stashed the boxes away and then discussed plans for selling the Fourth of July goods to local candy stores and other merchants.

Later as I said goodnight to Freddie, he took a few steps down the sidewalk, then turned and said, "Victor."

I stopped and turned around. "What you want?"

"You did a bang-up job tonight," he said with all seriousness.

We both burst out laughing and waved goodnight once again.

# 5

# RUMBLES, RIOTS, RAPES

Victor! Victor!" Henry, vice-president of the Roman Lords, ran into Pop's Candy Store, on the corner of Riverdale and Powell Streets. I looked up from sucking coke through a straw. Henry was in a state of panic. He shook me.

"One of the Jibaros is comin' up the block. He's got a rifle in his hand." The words rattled off his mouth in bullet speed fashion.

I stood up and stiffened. "He's got his nerve. We'll kill him! What's he doin' walking in daylight into our 'hood with a rifle?"

An olive-skinned Jibaro gang member burst in the door— just like in the movies. He came directly over to me, put the barrel of the rifle in my face and said, "Tell your man to tell your boys you better not come down in our territory anymore or there's gonna be a few dead Romans. And we don't like the smell of dead Romans. They stink." He spit on the floor.

Henry and I stood motionless staring at the rifleman. We dared not challenge him—he had the upper hand. After a few minutes he slowly backed out the door and backtracked to his own turf five blocks away. We went to the doorway and watched him disappear.

I was stunned for a moment, he had caught us by surprise.

The first cardinal rule in gang warfare, shock, and surprise, belonged to the Jibaros. It was now our task to plot a return maneuver.

I spotted my brother Ricky. "Come here, Ricky, right away. I need you. Run home as fast as you can and get the two guns." Before I could say another word his sneakers were pounding the pavement like a streak of lightning.

Suddenly he came to a full stop and yelled over his shoulder, "Where are they? Where are the guns in the house?"

"Under the gas range," I announced. The whole neighborhood could hear us shouting.

In two minutes he returned and handed over the guns like they were toys.

"Here, you use this one," I said to Henry, giving him the .38. I kept the 45 automatic for myself. Both guns were loaded—I always had them ready for such emergencies as these.

With guns in hand, we took off down the street after the rifleman. After a three-block walk, we were suddenly fired on. Ducking behind a car we saw the rifle barrel pointing out of a doorway a block ahead. Weaving in and out between cars, Henry and I pursued. He continued his fire. When we narrowed the distance between us to approximately a half a block, we opened fire in return. We both shot two bullets—hitting the side of a building.

Without realizing it we had gone into the Jibaro territory. Other members of their gang came in sight so we fired on them and they retreated. The rifleman disappeared, apparently hurrying to a rooftop for a better vantage point to shoot at us. I ran into the middle of the street and fired two or three more wild shots at the second and third-floor apartment windows. I screamed out, "Don't you ever forget the Roman Lords!"

Waving to Henry, I motioned for him to follow me back to our own turf. There we rushed around frantically trying to gather our members. Most of us were scattered. Some were not even in the neighborhood. We sent runners up and down the street, and up and down the many stairs of the apartment houses, knocking on doors scouting recruits. I sent the first two Roman Lords to the hideout for some weapons.

Since it wasn't an expected rumble, no plans were laid out in advance. Gang wars should be fought at a certain time and place, with fighting turf agreed upon mutually by the warlords or whoever is designated to make such arrangements. If it isn't, the battle could turn into a neighborhood brawl, with innocent people and children getting hurt—even shot. When that happened it often led to a full-scale riot.

After hustling together about thirty members, we went in a group toward Livonia Avenue—the undesignated territorial line (our 38th parallel) between the Roman Lords and the Jibaros. They, in turn, were there to meet us. We grouped on either side of the street, about half a block from Livonia. They were about the same distance on their side. We carefully inched toward the dividing line. On a given signal they suddenly charged us. We had baseball bats, clubs, pipes, and knives. We decided against the guns to keep from drawing the police. We had a go at each other, and then retreated behind our lines, regrouping for another charge. During one of the times of hand-to-hand combat, when we were in Jibaro territory, two of our guys, Benny and Oscar, got trapped and wrestled to the ground. Before we could defend them Oscar was knocked cold from a hit on the head with a baseball bat, and Benny was slashed with a knife on the head. The Jibaros scattered all the way back deep inside their turf, leaving us to take care of Benny and Oscar. We took Oscar to his home where his mother treated him, but we had to call an ambulance for Benny. He required seventeen stitches, in the hospital.

Such were the rewards of street gang warfare. We all knew it could just as well have been one of us. But we didn't have time to think about it. It was time to "get even." We dared not let the ugly beating of Benny and Oscar go by the boards. We knew, and they knew, it was the code of gang warfare to exact revenge.

We talked over when we should do it and how we should do it.

I chimed in, "We can't let them get away with it for a minute."

"I'm for goin' right now," someone else agreed. "Think of Benny there in the hospital now all cut up, while the Jibaros are probably over there laughing at us."

We didn't have to take a vote. I looked at Big Ray and suggested, "Knives?"

He quickly answered, "Yeah, the new ones in the hide- out." We both remembered at the same time that we had them stashed away from a robbery we had pulled in a warehouse. We sent three guys to get them.

We decided rather than sending a large contingent into their area, we would send two guys, hoping not to attract attention. They went over, grabbed a Jibaro and dragged him toward our turf. He screamed so loud and put up such a resistance we had to wrestle him to the ground before having a chance to get him over the border line. A group of us joined the act and started stomping, kicking, and punching him. Before we could do him much damage, the Jibaros came in full force. Outnumbered we had to retreat.

The next few hours we played cat and mouse games with each other. We made attempts to rush one of them and bring him inside our turf but were unsuccessful. We began exchanging gunshots which brought the police. Extra squad cars patrolled the streets forcing us to take refuge in hallways and rooftops. All we could do was wait it out. Perhaps the cops would leave.

It was now late afternoon and the cops remained in full force. We began getting nervous. The longer we were delayed getting revenge on the Jibaros the angrier we became, and the more time they had to plan a defense. The more we thought about Benny and Oscar the worse we felt. But still, the cops were in our way. As long as they were present we couldn't do a thing. All this was the topic of our conversation as we continued playing the waiting game.

"Let's forget about the pigs and go after them anyway," one of the guys suggested.

"And get caught in the middle with the police coming at us from one angle and the Jibaros from another? You're crazy," I said, knowing it was a foolhardy idea. "We just have to wait and be patient. Then we make our move."

For the next hour, we cooled it. Most of us were still on the rooftop, with a few stationed below in a position where we could signal each other. From above we could keep our eyes on both the police and the Jibaros. Time slowly dragged by.

Our waiting was interrupted by the sound of something heavy hitting the sidewalk. We rushed to the edge of the roof to see a policeman lying on the sidewalk, a refrigerator crashed on to the cement next to him. Two of our brainless dudes had decided to create some action. They had dropped a small refrigerator on the sidewalk, just barely scraping a policeman and knocking him unconscious.

Now we knew we were in real trouble. If the policeman died, one of us would get it for sure. If he lived we were still in trouble. One way or another they would find a Roman Lord, whoever happened to be at the wrong place at the wrong time, and they would mess him up something terrible.

In minutes, squad cars came from every direction. The word was spread that a policeman was in distress. It looked like all hell broke loose. Cops poured into the neighborhood with some immediately headed toward the rooftop spot where the refrigerator was dropped from.

We split.

Frankie, one of our rooftop lookout patrols, who had nothing to do with dumping the refrigerator but watched it all, was running to a hideout spot when he was caught by two policemen. They didn't ask questions. They clubbed him and dragged his body toward a patrol car. Frankie yelled, "Let me go! I didn't do it … I ain't your man!"

They weren't convinced. The word spread, "They got Frankie… the cops got Frankie… They're gonna kill him."

Like ripples, the information about Frankie vibrated throughout the neighborhood. It blew the lid off the whole block. With the tension that already existed and always did—and with the hate for the men in blue—the streets turned into a war zone. Bricks, bottles, garbage cans became missiles. Old and young alike reacted. Riot conditions prevailed. The police shot warning signals in the air with their guns. Reinforcements came in. Arrests were made.

Things didn't cool off completely till two or three o'clock in the morning.

The riot had serious repercussions. Our whole neighborhood went on the police wanted list. We were heavily patrolled for days. The police wore helmets or kept them close at hand as they drove back and forth, hour after hour. Groups of young adults, teens, and older men stood on the streets talking over every detail of the riots, and complaining about the conditions that caused it. Naturally, we only saw our side of the issue. When the patrol cars passed by, our tongues stopped wagging—all heads and eyes followed the path of the car until it turned the corner. In another fifteen minutes, it was back.

Occasionally there were episodes of garbage cans or bricks thrown off a rooftop, but we managed to do some of our own patrolling and controlling of tempers. We knew another riot would mean certain death for some of us.

Following the riot, it was dangerous to get stopped by the police in other neighborhood. If they asked us where we were from and we said Powell Street or any other street in our area, we were immediately associated with the riot and harassed, arrested or beaten. Our reputation followed us.

In the days and weeks following the riot, the neighborhood seemed to take a turn for the worse (if that was possible). The riot brought out the worst in us while unleashing pent-up anger. The police were the first and most available focal point upon which to vent our frustration.

I never remember hating any one particular policeman. We seemed to hate police in general—not a particular person. I am no sociologist or psychologist, but evidently New York's finest were representative of those persons or systems in society we felt caused us to be trapped in the ghetto. Of course, they didn't want to be there any more than we did. We were cast in a role of enemies in a jungle war neither side asked for or knew how to solve. The same war goes on today in cities throughout the country.

During these days the "Rape Game" started. Fortunately, I was never a party to it but the stories traveled in the neighborhood. Groups of guys began a crazy kick of raping girls and middle-aged women. They worked the dark alleys and streets and using a blanket, they threw it over the selected victim. Then they would wrap a rope around the blanket and take their victim to a rooftop. They would take turns raping her; using the blanket to cover her mouth to prevent screaming.

One night they dragged a woman to their familiar rooftop spot. They usually didn't know who they had until they laid the person down.

After several had committed the act of rape, one of the guys, whose turn was next, said, "I want a light."

"What for, you gonna burn her?" he was asked.

"No, man, I just want to see what we got," the young rapist answered.

"Why you got to see, fathead? If you see her, she'll see you. You want to be identified?"

"Yeah," another piped in, "he's right, man. You don't need a see—all you need to do is feel," He laughed.

"Look, you do it your way and I'll do it mine. I want a light. Pepe, come on, give me a match."

Pepe handed it to him. He lit the small book-match. The small flame broke the darkness ever so slightly.

Pepe let out a scream and jumped up. He held his head and wept and screamed.

"What's the matter with Pepe?" someone asked. "We just raped Pepe's mother."

In horror, the rest of the group looked on helplessly as Pepe ran to the edge of the building and leaped over. Rather than face the agony of having played the "Rape Game" with his very own mother, he ended his life.

# 6

# SON, PLEASE COME HOME

Between driving my car, pulling robberies, and keeping in good standing as the Sergeant-of-Arms with the Roman Lords—I lived a busy, exciting kind of life.

Nevertheless, a lot of time was spent "on the corner" doing nothing. Action and inaction was centered there. Gang rumbles were born, and often climaxed, on our favorite street corner. Serious romances or "puppy love" ignited there while fights and arguments were started and settled. Games to pass the time were invented and jokes told.

Epic stories were shared with many lies exchanged. When things became really boring, we just talked, drank cokes, and goofed off.

One April evening on this same corner, the world of hard drugs came to my attention when Diablo, Henry, and Little Louie walked to the corner where a group of us were chatting. They looked strange and acted stranger. One rubbed his nose while another kept running his hand over his face. Diablo went to the curb, bent over and vomited.

"What's wrong with Diablo—and the other two guys?" I asked.

One in the street corner group laughed. No one answered my question. I couldn't dig the scene. What was going on here?

"I know those guys are high," I finally said after careful observation. But I didn't know high with what or under what influence. It was as if a weird disease had overtaken them.

For several days, every time I saw them they were different. They were not themselves. They looked dreamy, "out of it," as someone observed.

I concluded it was some kind of drug. But I was certain it wasn't pot or pills.

"It's something stronger because of the way they act," I told a friend who, like me, didn't know what was going on.

"Yeah man—those dudes scare me. It's like they're there, but yet not really all there."

He went on to say, "I saw Diablo the other day in the candy store. He ain't the same no more. He looked weird—like a living ghost. He was sitting on one of the chairs and began to nod with his head up and down. He kept rubbing his nose—his lips seemed real dry. When he got up it looked like he was going to fall over but he never did."

It took me a while to discover the mysterious substance that caused their trance-like behavior. It turned out to be the hard stuff—heroin.

Until this time, drug addiction was the bag of the older guys. I knew very little about the problem—neither did most of the

Roman Lords. We were proud to be jitter-buggers, fighters, small-time robbers, and sometimes pot smokers—but dope addicts we were not.

Diablo, Henry, and Little Louie became the first victims. Diablo was turned on by his older brother. He, in turn, pushed it onto Henry and Little Louie. Unknown to the rest of the gang, they were "snorting," then later "skin popping." We tried to talk them out of it, but we had discovered their activity too late. They were "hooked." We left them alone and warned each other to stay clean, agreeing that as soon as anyone touched the hard stuff he was no longer a Roman Lord.

Our drug prevention program was unsuccessful. One by one I watched, first this one, then another, get hit by the curse of curiosity and sneak off to a "shooting gallery" to see what it was all about. Every day those of us who refused to turn on were approached, "Try it—you'll like it," they promised.

In a year's time there were dope fiends all over our neighborhood. I said many times to the clean guys, and the users, "You'll never get me on that junk. Not me—I'm going to watch myself. I have a future ahead of me."

I'd see the Roman Lords turned addicts and ridicule them. I said to Big Ray, "Look at those bums. What good are they hooked on that stuff? They're no good to the gang, no good to themselves, no good for nuttin'."

The drug situation frightened my parents. Dad would warn me day after day, "Don't you dare get involved in that dope stuff. Things are bad enough now."

I didn't need much lecturing. I had enough sense to see one had to be strong in mind and body to rumble in a gang war, to drive a car, and to plan and pull off robberies. I told Mom and Dad, "Don't worry about me, I'm too smart for that."

I meant it. I was dead serious. It was one of the few things my parents and I agreed on.

I felt badly when Diablo started mainlining. At first, I kept completely away from all my dope using friends. I considered them to be stupid weak people. Once l had looked up to and respected Diablo. Now I began to look down on him with disdain.

Diablo kept coming around coaxing me to use the drug with him. "Get out of here," I would say, getting angry and walking away. But soon I had few friends. Almost all of them were using drugs.

Diablo would come back repeatedly. "You don't know what it's like unless you try it," he would enticingly appeal to my own curiosity.

I kept putting him off.

Weeks later he saw me in the pool room and said, "How would you like to get straight?"

I looked at him. "What did he mean?" I asked myself.

"How would you like to forget about your hassles for a while? Like smoking grass, only about a thousand times better." He described a beautiful picture and an unusual sensation. As he talked, he invited me to follow him. We went to a rooftop corner about three buildings from my own. We arrived to find other addicts shooting heroin in their veins. It was my first such encounter with that scene. I watched for a while, then told Diablo, "I'm goin', man. This ain't for me."

"Wait, Victor," he coaxed. "Let me just give you a little taste. How you going to know if it's bad unless you try it? C'mon, just once. It can't hurt you trying it just one time."

I hesitated—and watched.

The others were still going through their ritual. I watched as they sucked water out of a coke bottle into an eye drop- per. They didn't sterilize the needle—I knew that was bad. The next guy used the same water for his injection.

The scene repulsed me. Yet I was curious. What was so great about that snow white powder that my closest friends were so interested in, more than the gang, more than girls, more than anything? Why would they rather prick their skin with a needle than cut the flesh of a Jibaro, a Liberty Boy, or a Frenchman?

I decided I had to find out for myself. "OK. I'll try it," I told Diablo. "Just once."

I knelt down beside him as the last guy in the circle completed his injection. Diablo prepared the needle for me. My heart sank. My legs trembled.

My heart pounded faster and faster as the water was mixed with the powder. Diablo took off his belt and tied it around my arm. He rubbed his hand quickly up and down the inside part of my arm. I learned later it was to enable him to find the best vein for the insertion of the needle.

One of the other addicts said, "Boy, he's got beautiful fresh veins. He can easily get a hit, Diablo."

Everyone around me was starting to "goof" on the rush of the heroin. They moved slowly. Their reactions were like a slow-motion movie picture. They looked at me with wide open eyes.

Diablo drew the liquid substance up into the dropper. Before he drilled the needle he looked me straight in the eye. I knew why they called him Diablo. The English translation meant devil. He got his nickname because he was mean and ugly looking. He was wicked with the knife in the gang. Now he would do anything for a shot of dope. I saw the devil in his eyes.

"You ready?" he asked but didn't wait for an answer. The point of the needle broke my flesh and was pushed into the arm. I turned my head. He squeezed the dropper—the substance went into the bloodstream. He jerked out the needle, slapped my arm, pulled it in a forward motion like a doctor after taking a blood sample, and said, "Just relax, Victor. Just take it easy and relax. Enjoy the high."

I heard one of the guys say, "Watch he doesn't fall on us." "I hope he doesn't overdose."

In seconds the powerful heroin ingredients ran through my body. It rushed through my entire bloodstream. A wave of heat went to my head. My heart beat faster and faster.

"Wow. This stuff is really something," I said.

A great sensation overcame me. I was in a state of euphoria. The addicts called it being "blasted," or the "sensation."

I began to feel sleepy and drowsy—in a state of semi-consciousness. Yet simultaneously, I felt good. I was feeling good and bad at the same time.

Then suddenly my stomach rejected the feeling and the drug. I threw up. My head was dazed. I said to Diablo, "This is too much for me. I can't take it." I held my hand on the wall balancing myself. Then I fell over into my vomit.

"You'll be all right," he assured me. "Everyone feels just like you do the first time."

I kept shaking my head. I got up and stood against the door at the top of the stairway leading onto the rooftop. I mumbled, "No good... no good. It's too much." I repeated it over and over again.

In a few minutes, the dizziness passed away somewhat. I gathered back my senses. At that moment I vowed to myself, "I'll never take another shot of heroin."

Fifteen minutes later I went downstairs and walked the streets trying to walk off the high. I ran into my cousin Sammy. I took one look at him and was shocked to find out that he was high just like I was.

"Where you been?" I asked Sammy in disgust.

At the same time, I was shooting my vein for the first time, Sammy had done the same. We were both shocked to find out what the other had done. We walked together discussing our experiences, promising one another that we would stay away from the "white horse."

It's strange how one forgets so quickly, the bad side of drugs and only the "high" is remembered; that imaginary, sensation-producing magic carpet that jets the user "up, up, and away" from reality and into Alice in Wonderland.

My vow to Sammy to stay away from heroin lasted a total of thirteen hours. The very next day Sammy and I got together and decided how, where, and when the next shot would take place. It was apparent the sickness was mild in comparison to the sensation. I wanted to capture that certain special feeling once again. I wasn't hooked.

No one gets hooked on one shot, at least physically, or so we are told by the experts. But in one shot I had opened the door to addiction. Heroin is like the devil; give him an inch and he'll take a mile. Give him a vein and he'll take a life. Let him prick your skin with a needle and he'll pluck your soul from sanity into hell.

I looked for Diablo. "Where can I get some stuff?" I asked, straight-faced.

He smiled—like the devil. "You liked it, didn't you? What did I tell you? I knew you would."

"Yeah, it was all right. I'd like to just take it a few more times. Where do I buy it?" I knew he wouldn't be giving me the next shot free. The stuff was too powerful to be cheap.

Diablo mentioned the name of Ralphie. We walked toward his apartment together. He explained about Ralphie who just moved into the neighborhood from Spanish Harlem. "Ralphie's got some real good connections and he pushes the best stuff around."

We knocked on apartment Number 9B.

The door opened a crack. A face stared out at us behind the chained door. "What you want?" the voice said to Diablo. Then he noticed me. "I told you never to bring anyone up here unless I know him."

Ralphie was angry. "It's all right. You can trust me—and this dude. Treat him nice. He's a brand new customer.

"He'll probably do a big business with you." The door opened. Ralphie looked me over.

"You got stuff?" Diablo asked.

Then turning to me Diablo asked, "You got bread? Give him your five," as he held out his hand.

I pulled out a five. In the other pocket was a roll of fives, tens, and twenties. I was loaded. The stealing business had life. Let him prick your skin with a needle and he'll pluck your soul from sanity into hell.

I looked for Diablo. "Where can I get some stuff?" I asked, straight-faced.

He smiled—like the devil. "You liked it, didn't you? What did I tell you? I knew you would."

"Yeah, it was all right. I'd like to just take it a few more times. Where do I buy it?" I knew he wouldn't be giving me the next shot free. The stuff was too powerful to be cheap.

Diablo mentioned the name of Ralphie. We walked toward his apartment together. He explained about Ralphie who just moved into the neighborhood from Spanish Harlem. "Ralphie's got some real good connections and he pushes the best stuff around."

We knocked on apartment Number 9B.

The door opened a crack. A face stared out at us behind the chained door. "What you want?" the voice said to Diablo. Then he noticed me. "I told you never to bring anyone up here unless I know him."

Ralphie was angry. "It's all right. You can trust me—and this dude. Treat him nice. He's a brand new customer.

He'll probably do a big business with you." The door opened. Ralphie looked me over.

"You got stuff?" Diablo asked.

Then turning to me Diablo asked, "You got bread? Give him your five," as he held out his hand.

I pulled out a five. In the other pocket was a roll of fives, tens, and twenties. I was loaded. The stealing business do what one once did. Then it was three per day, then four, sometimes more. Suddenly I realized I was hooked. It happened when I ran out of money to score. One day after taking the morning fix, I had nothing for the afternoon.

By three o'clock I wasn't feeling good at all. The shakes came over me. I got sicker and sicker. Perspiration poured off my forehead and desire burned in me. Then it dawned on me, "You're hooked, Victor. You've got the monkey on your back. You're a junkie just like the rest of them." I knew it was true. I could not function without a fix.

I went home to sleep it off. I didn't know any better. I learned withdrawal was not like shaking a cold or the flu. In thirty minutes I was up and out looking for the medicine man.

"Give me a taste," I asked a junkie I knew slightly. He said he didn't have anything. I asked a few others and got the same response.

"Please. Give me just a little taste," I began begging. My hand started shaking.

I had no bread, no heroin, and no friends. I got sicker by the minute.

"Can't you see I'm sick?" I pleaded with Diablo when I finally found him. I was relieved to see him. I was sure he would fix me up.

No dice. Not even my close friend Diablo would have pity on my pain-riddled body. His rejection was worse than the craving. I realized what dope did to us. It was no longer the brotherhood of the gang—the companionship of street buddies—the sharing of neighborhood cliques. Now it was every man—every junkie—for himself. There was no time to care, to share, to lend a hand. We were too sick, too busy scoring, or too "high" to care.

I kept going from one junkie to the next. "I'll do anything for a fix," I told myself. For the first time, I was even willing to kill for the drug.

Finally, an older addict told me, "You can get rid of those shakes for a while if you get some Cosenil cough syrup. It costs only sixty-five cents. Drink it all down at once. You'll feel better."

It did help get me through the night. But the next morning I was sick again and desperate for a fix. I broke into an apartment house and stole a television set. I sold it on the streets for twenty dollars. I was set for another day.

For one solid year, I shot junk. My daily routine was to shoot up, steal, shoot up, and steal again. In between, I did enjoy a temporary "high." It didn't last long and I knew I would soon have to be out "hustling" for more money, or I might be sick; so I made the most of every fix.

One kick I got when under a heavy dose of heroin was staying up all night watching television and playing the "rat game." The game consisted of setting up a special rat trap. I tied a strong cord to a garbage can, turned it upside down, and lifted it a few inches off the kitchen floor by wrapping the cord around the radiator for leverage.

I strung the cord from the kitchen to my bedroom. Bait consisted of tuna fish in wrapping paper, placed directly under the garbage can.

While waiting, I kept the cord pulled and watched television, listening for the rustling of the paper—the signal that my prey was in the trap. I lowered the garbage can over the rat by letting up on the cord.

Having caught my game, I put on rubber gloves, took the rat to the bathroom, tied a string around him, sat down on a chair, and slowly lowered the creature into the water until he was drowned.

I played the game all night (my record was eight rats), first identifying with the rat—since I was living like an animal myself—but then drowning them in revenge for the times as a little guy I had to chase them from my room.

I shot dope to feel good enough to steal, and I needed to steal to pay the cost of the fix. Then I noticed I wasn't getting the good "sensation" anymore. I had to fix just to stay normal, just to keep from getting sick. Dope became my medication instead of my pleasure.

Mom and Dad discovered I was a user about eight months after I started mainlining. Many addicts managed to hide it from their families much longer. But my parents were aware—or made themselves aware—of dangers such as narcotics. They looked for the signs. They could see the changes in my behavior patterns. I dressed sloppily. I ate little. I didn't care. I wouldn't talk to them and I ignored my brother and sister.

They reacted severely. I'm glad they did. Some guys had no one who cared if and when they got hooked. They had nobody to get after them—no one to plead for them to stop.

After my parents knew the whole story of my addiction, I would walk in the house and Dad would say, "Here comes the demon."

I even stooped so low as to steal from them. My Mom couldn't keep her purse around or I'd steal all her money. I would even rob my own brother.

"What are you doing to us?" Father would ask. "You may as well put a knife or a bullet in us. You're killing your old man and old lady."

He continued his rant, "We watch what you're doing to yourself. We can't stand it, seeing our very own son turning into an animal, a thief, and a dirty dope addict. You can't keep doing this to yourself and to us. Do you want your brother or your baby sister to grow up a junkie too?"

Over and over again I heard the same routine. Dad would threaten. Mom would plead. Most of those times, I was too sick to hear or to even care. On occasion, I'd listen to Mom's pleading but wouldn't react one way or another.

Once I walked into the apartment and Dad yelled, "Why don't you stay away and leave us alone?"

I swore at him, "You give me five bucks and I will leave." He pointed toward the door, "Get out! Get out! Don't you dare ask for a penny from us!"

I jumped up, turned the kitchen table over and looked at Mom, "Please, before I do something drastic—give me some money."

"I'm sorry, son. You heard your father. I don't have a dime to give you," she answered.

I started arguing with my dad, upset that he wouldn't allow Mom to help. I screamed at him, "You can go to hell!" and stormed into the living room, pulling the lamp cord out of its socket.

"I'm going to sell the lamp and get straight," I yelled. Dad took a swing at me and I threw the lamp down and tried to tackle him to the floor, but fell down myself.

"You see what I mean?" He stood over me speaking to Mom. "This boy is a demon. I don't think even God could change his life. He's going to destroy himself and take us with him. I can't take this any longer."

His anger had reached its boiling point. While he spoke, Mother was beside herself with uncontrolled emotion.

I looked up from the floor at the scene—but now all feeling was gone. Heroin was still first. There was no room for sorrow, shame or, anything else.

Mother was a practicing Christian and a regular church goer. After learning of my addiction, she increased her church attendance and even began prayer meetings in the house.

"Please pray for my son," was her constant request, whether at the home prayer meetings or at church. Unlike many parents, she had no room for shame. The situation was desperate and she knew only God could intervene.

I had rejected God and renounced the church and religion, yet Mom kept believing that someday God would change my life and give me peace. Thankfully, she never let me forget it. Like a detective pursuing a suspect, she trailed me with her message of hope.

While shooting pool one day at the neighborhood hang out, one of the guys caught my attention, "Victor, your old lady's here." I looked up from eyeing the number five ball to see the little woman who had become my shadow. I was embarrassed in front of my friends.

She walked right over to me and spoke, "Son, I want you to come home." She grabbed my arm and tried to pull me with her.

"Ah, go home, Mom," I said bitterly, and continued to ignore her.

I would stay away two, three, and sometimes four days at a time. When I did, she came looking for me. She'd ask anyone and everyone, "Have you seen my boy? Have you seen my drug-addict son, Victor?"

She always managed to find me no matter how long I was gone or where I was. I would hear the familiar words, "Son, please come home." She followed me through alleyways, backyards, into dirty basements—and on to the rooftops; even if they were blocks away from our building. I don't think there was a mother quite like mine. She refused to give up. And she never stopped pleading, "Son, please come home."

Once she found me on a rooftop just as an argument was ensuing over a misunderstanding between me and the other drug addicts who accused me of beating them out of some money. They had knives and switchblades, so I tangled with them the best I could. But I couldn't fight like I once had. I was a bag of bones. They wrestled me to the ground and were carrying me to the edge of the roof, to throw me off, when at the exact time my Mom was praying in the kitchen. She heard a voice, she heard the voice of the Lord say "Victor is in trouble, go up to the roof top." Mom arrived on the scene. She rushed right into the middle of the chaos to defend me—and I managed to break out of their grasp and run.

People said to Mom, "You're wasting your time with Victor. Don't chase him around." But, she would not be denied. She refused to see her son lost to heroin and the devil—without a fight. No matter what hour I came home, day or night, I would find her praying; and it was always for me.

During one of those prayer meetings, I came home stoned as usual. It was three a.m. and I thought everyone would be in bed. Turning on the light in the living room, I saw Mom on her knees. She would make any space in our tiny apartment her Prayer Room. She didn't look up from petitioning the Almighty on my behalf. I passed by her and lay down on my bed. I resented her prayers—no doubt due to the conviction and guilt I felt both toward her and God.

"Oh God, save my son," I could hear her words. "Give him a new life. Give us a new son. Listen to my prayer. Please, God. You are our only hope of salvation." She went on addressing God as if he were right in the room sitting down on the couch next to her.

She finished her prayer and looked in my room to see if I had come in. She came over and put her arms around me and started to weep. I rolled over away from her. "You're a crazy woman. Why do you pray like that? You're wasting your breath if you think God is going to help me." I was very bitter as I poured out my frustration and rebellion on her.

"The only thing that's going to give me peace is maybe dying of an overdose or getting shot by a cop!" I yelled.

She pulled me towards her and looked me straight in the eye. I'll never forget how she spoke from the bottom of her heart and with the voice of authority as she prophesied, "Son, I don't care what you say or what society says. I know deep inside you, you want to be different. God is going to get a hold of you one of these days. You are going to be transformed by His power."

"Please don't pray for me anymore," I responded.

# 7

# TREATMENT WORSE THAN THE STREETS

What happened to you?" I asked Sammy, looking at his bandaged head.

"My old man hit me," he said as we walked along together, his eyes glued to the ground.

"Hit ya, with what?" I asked.

"A hammer, that's what," his voice was subdued.

"A hammer, what was he trying to do? Kill you?" I questioned with sympathy.

"He was mad enough to do it. He told me if I didn't go to the hospital or someplace else for help, he would kill me next time. Hell, Victor—he's serious. I've never seen my old man like that before."

Sammy related a problem both of us had in common. Every drug addict faces the turmoil of broken family relationships—mothers whose hearts are broken, fathers upset and angry, and both confused as to what to do.

Other members of the family—brothers, sisters, and relatives—were also affected emotionally, and sometimes directly influenced to use drugs. I knew quite a few married guys who started their wives on drugs—some solely for the purpose of creating a drug craving in them so they would prostitute their bodies to get money for drugs for both of them.

Unfortunately, what parents do when they discover a son or daughter on dope is panic and allow their emotions to take over their logic. It's real easy to do. Naturally one gets angry. Most of the time parents are angry at them- selves or embarrassed, and many times they don't realize their own reactions. They feel a deep sense of failure as parents. Some blame it on anything but themselves (friends, the school, someone put a drug in their coke, the community). Others admit personal guilt but often go into deep depression. There are some who deny they are angry at themselves and vent their frustration and despair on the addicted child. Those who panic and lose their heads end up making matters worse—like Sammy's father hitting him with a hammer. When parents overreact they cause the child to retreat, lines of communication are broken, and rebellion sets into the heart of the child. This usually increases the need for drugs—if nothing more than to escape the emotional trauma that exists.

Parents must face the reality of the situation. They have a duty to believe their child is "hooked" and be cautious not to play the role of the enabler. I have seen too many parents disregard the warning signals (whether it is drug usage or any other kind of behavior problem). Their attitude is to ignore the problem and hope it will go away. They wear blindfolds. They are either too busy to see something is wrong or too alienated to know when their child's behavioral patterns are changing which only worsens the situation. Perhaps if they could see trouble coming, or see it developing, something could be done before addiction or other troubles set in.

In my case it probably wouldn't have done my parents any good discovering my drug abuse in its early stages. The die had already been cast before I smoked the first reefer, or took the first bag of dope. Drugs were the final symptom of my troubles.

Many ask, "What can be done by parents in such a situation?" Unfortunately, the answer is, "Nothing." If this sounds pessimistic, it is. As far as doing something to directly help some kids stop taking drugs, it can't be done more times than it can. But, there are other ways in which a family, parents or spouses can help. They can hold on and never give up hope. Most importantly, they should not do anything that will cause their relationship with the child to suffer permanent damage and alienation. Too many parents force their children into programs before they are ready. Many throw them out of the house and sever all contact, or refuse to accept phone calls or visits after they have left home. Still, others refuse to visit them if they become incarcerated. All these reactions add insult to injury.

My mother kept after me. She never gave up. I ignored her, was rude, and even made fun of her—yet this did not dissuade her. When I was angry with her, I was really angry with myself.

It would do parents well if they would realize when dealing with their children, that oftentimes what their children say or do often is just the opposite from what they mean. The addict's hostility may just be a cover up for loneliness and a desire to be helped. Their action is a signal for help.

A teenager running away from home may just be trying to see if Mom and Dad will miss him. I know of one guy who came home "high" every night. And, every night his mother hollered at him.

One evening when he returned in his usual state, she didn't say a word. He went to his room and said, "My mother must not love me anymore—she quit hollering at me."

Sammy and I sat in the park discussing our mutual parental problems. We decided to go to the hospital together to "kick" our habit. I had heard about a hospital on 100th Street in Manhattan that opened a special ward for addicts. A new experimental program was in operation to give drug addicts a new drug called methadone. It helped the addict detoxify. It is a synthetic heroin substitute to relieve the withdrawal pains.

Sammy and I were two of the first to go on this program. Back then, the doctors promised a cure, something they still do today. Methadone was the new answer to the drug addicts' problem—a so-called magic, scientific, medical cure. There were predictions of the junkie disappearing from the streets. When an addict is on methadone—which can be taken in tablet or liquid form (drinking it in orange juice)—his drug craving is satisfied; that is, his physical drug craving. If he tries to shoot heroin, he can't get high.

It sounded too good to be true. It wasn't true then, and still isn't today. Now addicts are getting hooked on methadone. It is often worse than kicking heroin—virtually impossible for those having been using it over a long period of time.

The original concept of the methadone treatment was for the addict to take it for a period of time, and then stop.

While under maintenance, he would receive psychiatric treatment, vocational training, and other supportive assistance—all designed to get to the root of his problem; to find out what got him hooked in the first place while teaching him to deal with his problems. The hope was that he would no longer have a need for the drug.

It didn't work. As soon as the addicts stopped methadone they went right back to drugs. The mental habit was still there. The addict still had something wrong inside him.

Methadone alleviated the drug craving but not the cause for the addiction. And many of them found other ways to beat methadone and get high on other sources.

Now addicts are permanently maintained on methadone. Some are sincerely motivated to stay off heroin and seem to be helped by methadone use. They can work, live with their families, and quit their life of crime and street hustling. But they are still addicts. And, they must go through life classified as incurables. Statistically, no one knows the physical damage being done to their bodies by the continual consumption of the chemical components of the methadone drug. I'm afraid the treatment may be worse than the addiction.

I also believe the use of methadone as the major drug cure by the government and society is an admission of total failure of the "system" in the rehabilitation of the addict. It tells the addict, "You cannot be cured. You are a sick person. And, since you are an invalid we must maintain you in your state of addiction for the rest of your life."

Sammy and I did not know what we were getting into. Luckily, Sammy was allergic to methadone. But they gave it to me for fourteen days and then stopped. There was no maintenance program then.

By the third week, I began feeling better. I told Sammy I was going to "make it', and hoped to return to high school and finish my education. I had new desires—and I began to hope again. Drugs had beaten me down too many years. I wanted out, I was tired of being an addict. The highs were great, but I couldn't take the lows anymore. I had enough of the sickness, the cold-turkey in jail, along with the criminal style of living to get a fix. I despised the hours waiting on a street corner for the drug connection to show up when my dope supply ran out, and the hassle with my parents—I was sick of it. I thought about the money I had to raise to keep my veins fed: $25 to $50 a day—$200 a week—$1,000 a month—$12,000 and more a year.

I sat at the window of the hospital looking down on Manhattan's East Side highway. As the cars sped along I watched them as I wondered and dreamed.

"Look at those people," I told Sammy. "They're free. They can go where they want to go. They can do what they want to do. They're free—and human. I want to be like that," I said daydreaming out loud.

It was hard to keep from thinking about dope. No matter where the conversation started among the group of us addicts in the hospital, we eventually got back to our favorite subject— heroin. As much as we talked about quitting, we still ended up talking about it—and mentally shooting up dope in our heads while we did. Everything we talked about reminded us of dope.

I learned a lot in the hospital—a lot about drugs, crime, and the street life. All of us compared notes. We shared our experiences like where we procured our drugs and who the good pushers were. We talked about methods of getting money pointing out the good neighborhoods, stores, or apartments to rob and which cops to look out for. I also got an education about what pills to take to get high when we couldn't get heroin and what drugstores to buy black market "bennies," "reds," and "yellow jackets."

It was a drug addict's seminar. It was impossible to keep away from dope even in the hospital. Guys checked out one day and returned the next saying they were going to visit a patient. They brought in drugs. A guy named Caesar came to the gate of our ward one day and called out, "Hey dudes, look here. I got presents for you." Before we turned and saw who it was, pills hit the floor, rolling in all directions.

"Oh boy, somebody loves us." We all dashed pell-mell after the red, white and yellow pills.

"Caesar is a Santa Claus. Bless him."

The guards called for help, but before they could do anything the floor was cleaned, and the pills were sliding down throats.

There were other temptations as well. We had some male nurses who were homosexuals. They made constant passes and would offer to provide free drugs for spending a night with one in the storage room. Even some of the police guards were homosexual. Every day I was propositioned to have homosexual relations with one of them. So, instead of them guarding me, I had to guard myself. The consequence of not accepting their advances meant I got no favors.

When it was time to go home, I was overjoyed—for more reasons than one. "The hospital is worse than the streets," I told Sammy after we were finally discharged. The doctor and psychiatrist pronounced us cured. On a Friday morning, I returned to Brownsville.

That night I tried to sleep but found that without methadone I couldn't rest. My bones ached and I was sick. It was like kicking a habit all over again. As I tossed and turned wrestling with the pain—my hopes slowly faded with each passing hour.

"I'm not cured. I'm still a dope addict," I said to myself and knew it was so. I was now hooked on methadone. The doctors only exchanged one habit for another. They changed a dollar bill into four quarters—it still came out the same. I was a dope addict.

At one o'clock in the morning, after everyone was asleep, I couldn't take it any longer and got out of bed. Mother heard me.

"Where are you going, Victor," she asked as we met at the door.

"I can't sleep, Mom. That hospital did something to me. It made me worse." I gave her my sad story. She pleaded with me to stay home.

"Don't go out there. You're clean, son. You don't need that stuff."

I walked down the stairs. She stood watching me disappear into the night—and back into the world of drug addiction. She knew it was useless to beg. Once the urge came, nothing, or no one—not even a mother's tears, pleading, or begging—could prevent me from getting that cherished fix.

"Cooker here I come...cooker here I come," the words raced over and over in my mind. I rushed down the dark street to Ralphie's. His was a twenty-four-hour business. In twenty minutes I injected myself. And 21 days of treatment went down the gutter in one $5 bag of dope. With it went my dreams—snuffed out in my euphoric state.

"Why fight it?" I justified my return to the bag. "You're an addict, and you'll always be one." I concluded I was only accepting the inevitable.

For seven years the same misery-go-round continued, at a cost of approximately $75,000. Fourteen times I returned to the hospital, not for a cure—just to dry out. After shooting heroin for a number of months the physical system builds up tolerance and immunity. More and more drugs are needed to get high. The daily cost soars to $50 or more. That is when going to the hospital helps. Fourteen days of drying out and detoxification purifies the system. This lets one bag last the whole day. We used the hospital to stop the tolerance cycle. With all the money it costs to run the drug detoxification division of the hospital and to have the addict use it for such, amounts to an astronomical sum. Now methadone is used to accomplish the same.

Knowing there was no cure for my addiction, I tried other avenues. Time after time my parents tried everything they could. "I can kick the habit but not here, a new environment is what I need," I told my parents. I convinced them to send me back to Puerto

Rico. "I'll have new friends, a new environment, and a new start." They agreed because of their desperation to help and it sounded like a good idea.

However, my problem went with me, since the trouble was not the dope in my body—it was the dope in Victor. It was the dope of sin, of hate, and corruption in my heart. It went with me to Puerto Rico, it went with me in and out of rehab, doctors' offices, clinics. I was the same person inside. Within two weeks I was back to the same routine. Like a magnet, I gravitated to the same level of addiction.

I, like so many who think a new environment, new home, new school, new job, new friends or girlfriend, a new marriage, or even a new religion will change them, only fool ourselves. An addict, alcoholic, or other habit-bound person, lives with so many false hopes.

I was sincere. I wanted out. I had the desire and the will to change—but not the power to change. I deceived myself. I had faith and hope only in myself. But, I was morally, spiritually, and mentally bankrupt. There was nothing within me able to produce change. The power of positive thinking is all right if you have something positive to draw upon or plug into. I didn't. Most people in my condition don't. I needed something to couple with my will—something into which I could plug my will and motivation. Mom kept telling me if I had the will, God had the power. My will—His power. I couldn't get it and continued living on false hopes.

I sought the easiest way out. My kind always does. I looked for the shortest route to success; a way that has no pain, no suffering, no work, no waiting, and no price to pay. Up until now, I acquired this from the use of dope. When you feel bad—pop a pill, smoke grass, trip out, drink, or shoot up. Like magic the problem is gone—or at least covered up. Then when it comes to seeking a cure, the addict wants it the same way—instantaneously; a drug-like answer to a drug-taking problem. The doctor, psychiatrist, and others involved with addiction very often perpetuate this same attitude. They baby us. They do everything for the patient. He is never allowed to suffer or to experience pain. They remove from him the opportunity for personal commitment and responsibility in having a part in effecting his own cure.

I returned from Puerto Rico hooked after ending up in jail in their cold and crude incarceration facilities. I decided once again to return to the hospital. This time I was deter- mined I would take no medication.

After looking in the eyes of my younger brother and sister, Ricky and Ellie I knew I had to change. "Lock me up in a room, doc. I'm going cold turkey. I've got to do this for myself, I have the will now" I said convincingly enough to have him let me do it.

"After withdrawal let me see the shrink (psychiatrist) to see if he can get my head together," I further instructed him.

"You'll have to sign papers giving us the right not to give you medication," he informed me. "You must do this at your own risk."

"I'll sign," I said.

The room they gave me had one single bed, a dresser, and a basin. "I'll need it for throwing up," I thought to myself. The one window had screens over it. Other drug patients must have tried to escape through the window, necessitating the window security.

I was all right the first few hours. My last fix kept me together. I slept off and on. Then, as I expected and was ready for, the cramps, chills, and body aches began. First, there were the cold chills, then hot ones, then cold ones again. I wrapped blankets around me, but still shivered like an epileptic. Minutes later I was hot again. First I was in bed, then out, then in again. While I was up I paced the floor. The hours dragged. Night was always the worse time—quiet and eerie like. There was no one to talk to, no one to help pass the time—to get my mind off the pain. I saw the clock outside my room on the corridor wall—it moved ever so slowly. The pain was worse than I had expected. My habit and the strength of the drugs I had been using were stronger than I calculated, and my system reacted accordingly. The more powerful the drug used, the more powerful the withdrawal pains.

The physical reaction was agonizing. The shakes increased. My bones felt like ice cubes. But the mental torment was worse than the physical suffering. One thought plagued my mind—DOPE. I had visions and illusions of a bag of dope before me.

"If I only had one—even a half a bag," I desperately wished. Drug scenes passed rapidly through my head. I pictured myself on rooftops getting ready for a drilling session. I imagined the match lighting the cooker, the beautiful white diluted powder heating, the dropper drawing it up, then the cure going into my veins. I could actually feel the sensation—the rush going down the system of roadways in my body. Oh, the sensation! I dreamed and tormented myself with wishful thinking. I would have given anything, even my right arm, to experience a fix of heroin at that moment.

But it was only a dream—an illusion, a desperate dope addict's imagination working double overtime. I wasn't on the rooftop. I wasn't about to cure my body of the agony. I was confined to four walls, a bed, and to kicking "cold turkey."

# 8

# A WHITE HANKIE

Dreams turned to nightmares—real ones. At four o'clock in the morning, I crawled out of bed soaked with perspiration.

"I can't take this anymore," I told myself. I wanted to die and I made a gallant effort to do so.

Standing at one wall, I ran full speed across the room banging myself into the opposite wall—head first. The impact bounced me to the floor. I then picked myself up and staggered across the floor back onto the hard cement. I took a second shot at it, but this attempt knocked me semi-unconscious.

I lay on the cold floor feebly moaning as my head kept spinning. I cried weakly at first, then louder and louder, "I want to die...I want to die...please let me die!"

A pool of blood gathered on the floor around my face as I bled from the cut on my mouth.

Ironically, my cries for death saved my life. Other patients on the floor heard the cries and called for help. A doctor came and gave me a shot of Spirene which knocked me out. A nurse then cleaned the wounds.

The next day I was greeted by the doctor and a wheelchair. As they helped me into it, I noticed a small mirror in the nurse's hand. As she handed it to me, the doctor said with disgust in his voice, "Take a good look at yourself."

I could hardly believe my eyes. I quickly turned my head aside.

"Oh God, what did I do?" I gasped. I laid my head on my shoulder and wept because I looked like a monster. My face was completely disfigured; the nose, mouth, and head were swollen and lacerated.

The doctor and nurse walked out leaving me to my tears and sorrow. For the first time, I called on God, "Help me, God. Look what I've done to myself. I need your help."

Three weeks later I forgot about God and my brush with death. I left the hospital, not to stay clean—but to get high. My mother knew it, she knew something was wrong with me. "Victor, is everything okay? Are you high again?" I looked with discontent towards her and said, "Not high enough."

I stopped every drug addict on the street asking the same question, "Where's Pancho? Where's Ralphie?" No one knew—or would tell me. Pancho was my main man—the best connection in the neighborhood. Ralphie ran a close second and I really needed them now. My return from the hospital to the streets was a rude awakening to the bad news that was plaguing the neighborhood. It was known as "panic."

This genuine panic was created when the "feds" or "narcos" cracked down and arrested a top-line drug dealer which resulted in the confiscation of a large haul of narcotics. The street supply dried up, and the street pushers ran out of stock. The effect on all the junkies was complete desperation.

Girls that were once beautiful had become victims of the streets, devastated by the addiction. They were crouched up in alleys, waiting for their next high.

Everyone gets hurt during times of panic. The addict can't get his usual three, four, five, or six bags of dope, so the doctors and drugstores get robbed, mugged, or even murdered as the drug-crazed junkies try to substitute other drugs to satisfy their need for a fix. The average citizen gets hurt because they too get mugged, robbed, or stabbed by the addict who gets so sick he will do almost anything to get money to pay the inflated price of $15 to $20 for a fix—if and when he can buy a bag at all. Fortunately for the addicts, the big drug dealers are good at their business, and soon the stuff flows abundantly on the streets again and panic time passes.

I searched high and low for Pancho. I knew if anyone had a few bags available it would be him. He ran a good business. His small corporation was comprised of himself and his girlfriend. He turned her onto stuff (I remembered when she was a pretty teenage girl in the neighborhood who never got into trouble), then taught her how to hustle money by prostituting. She was known to have gone out with almost every junkie, as well as every single (and some married) males on the block. While his woman worked the streets, Pancho stayed home with their three children. Women's lib would have liked Pancho—he did the dishes and in his own way cleaned up the house.

During times of panic even Pancho had to hit the streets. When I found him I asked, "Hey, man, you're a sight for sore eyes. Got anything?"

"You got to be kidding. Where you been, man? There ain't nothin' out here," he answered. We talked about other possibilities, and of teaming up together to score.

We got into an argument because he wanted to go to Harlem and see what was available, but I knew his children were alone at home. I didn't want him to leave them. "You've got a little baby there, you know, Pancho. You can't just leave like that," I reminded him.

He looked at me surprised. "So what, man, what do you care? It's my kid, not yours. I can do what I please...anyway, it's none of your business."

"I may be a junkie, Pancho, but at least I got some feeling left in this dope addict's heart." I was angry and as surprised as Pancho that I did care about his kids.

"You got awful righteous in the hospital. What did they do to you?" Pancho asked. Then he just walked away.

I went to his apartment and took his baby and went home.

"Where did you steal that baby?" my bewildered mother asked, perhaps wondering what new scheme I was involved in.

I explained the situation. She bathed the baby, changed the diaper (which hadn't been changed for several days), then persuaded me to return the baby to Pancho's apartment. I wished I had never brought him back.

A few months later while Pancho and his wife were out buying and selling dope their apartment caught on fire, and the baby burned to death.

A drug addict usually expresses very little feeling about anything—except his dope. But the death of Pancho's baby shook me. I sat around the house for days thinking—and feeling guilty as though I had had something to do with the death. In the months since my hospital ordeal, I had gotten "hooked" again, but I stayed clean for a few days so I could attend the baby's funeral.

After this event, I needed a special high—one that would help me to erase those experiences and feelings out of my mind.

I returned home and while walking through the kitchen to my room, my Mom suddenly stopped me and placed a white handkerchief on my chest. I was startled. "What is this all about? What is she trying to do?" I wondered.

Mom was crying—and praying. "Thank you, Lord, for answering my prayer. I place this anointed handkerchief on Victor's body in faith for my son's healing."

I could do nothing but stand and watch—and wonder. Lately, I had listened when Mom prayed and preached— and pleaded with me. I even began showing a little more interest in hearing about Mom's God. Maybe he was my way out. Although I didn't know what the handkerchief business was all about, I was touched. Her actions were so intense I felt strange inside—but couldn't interpret my own feelings.

I went to my room and found Ricky lying down. "Ricky, what's this hankie Mom put on my chest?" I asked.

"Mom went to this real big open air service yesterday and the evangelist prayed over the white handkerchief and told her to place it on your heart as a sign of faith—so you would be saved," was his explanation.

I shook my head and lay down—staring at the ceiling. Poor Mom, I thought. She'll try anything. I felt both sorrow and respect for her. I couldn't conceive that prayer over a white hankie could do any good. To me, it was like my visit to a spiritualist and medium who tried black magic and voodoo on me. Black magic hadn't worked— how could white magic?

# 9

# BORN AGAIN

Mom approached me one day with excitement and hope in her voice. "I found a new drug program where you can go for help, Victor."

She could see I was wearing down. All the changes I had gone through finally made me ready to do something— anything to get the monkey off my back.

"Where is it?" I asked.

"Right here in Brooklyn. A place called Teen Challenge. We just learned about it."

She continued to describe it in glowing adjectives, trying her best to build it up in my mind.

"OK, Mom. I'll go see what it's all about. I'll give it a try," I halfheartedly promised. My thoughts were that Teen Challenge was a special hospital for drug addicts.

At 9 o'clock the next morning Mom woke me and announced that both she and Dad would accompany me to this place they talked about.

Crawling out of bed I mumbled, "I gotta get straight first. I want a fix. I can't get on the subway like this. I'm too sick."

Mom did her best to convince me otherwise but found herself desperate to see me better. "Here's five dollars. Go do what you have to, but please promise me you'll return."

"I will. I promise you, Mother. I'll not let you down this time," I said, pulling on my pants and getting excited about the fix.

Outside I made a quick purchase and returned to the bathroom to feed my arm. Now I was ready. As always with stuff inside me I felt as if I could conquer the world—or at least my habit. The addict is truly "in a fix." He has to get "high" to think about getting down and clean. So he uses heroin in order to get himself into the frame of mind to get cured. Unfortunately, this only perpetuates his addiction.

The subway ride took about twenty minutes to get us to the Eighth Avenue Independent Subway stop at Clinton and Washington. The neighborhood, I noticed, was much like our own. We walked into a two-story brick building with tall, white pillars on the porch. In the lobby, I heard singing. I tried to figure out just where I was. The singing sounded like church. This isn't a hospital, I concluded.

A young man walked over, "Hi, I'm Mario. God bless you. It's good to have you here."

As soon as he said, "God bless you," I knew it wasn't a medical facility—and he was no doctor.

This is a church. These people are a bunch of crazy religious fanatics, I bet. Mom tricked me! I boiled with anger inside.

"Come on in the office," said Mario, as he began to pull me along before I was aware of what was happening. In the office, another young man in a sweatshirt sat behind a desk. I took a seat and eyed him closely. He looks familiar, I thought. Where have I seen him?

He offered his hand and I shook it.

"God bless you. What's your name?" he asked. I told him.

He introduced himself, "Well, I'm Nicky Cruz," and started to explain what the program was all about and how I could be cured. Then he started to preach. I just sat...looked...and stared.

The guy is cracked, I thought. He don't look like' no minister, yet he talks just like my old lady. He must be one of those hallelujah fanatics. I analyzed the situation and thought I had it figured out.

He kept talking while I kept analyzing. But I ran out of analyzing before he ran out of preaching, so I listened.

Speaking in Spanish, he said, "You think you can't be cured. I know you do. I know that's what you're thinking. That's not so. There is a positive cure to drug addiction. Jesus Christ is the man who can do it. He's the only one. Forget anything else."

He went on, "It ain't gonna work on your own. But, you probably know that by now—or you should. Are you desperate? Do you really want help? God's power can change you."

He spoke in rapid-fire fashion. "But, if you decide to come into this program, you can't be accepted now."

"Why not?" I asked puzzled.

"Cause you're high—I can tell. You have to come in here sick."

I wondered what he meant. How could I come in clean? Then he instructed me not to take a shot in the morning before coming into the Center.

I didn't like that and said to myself, "If that's what you got to go through to get to God—forget it."

I felt like saying, "You can hang it on the wall, preacher boy," but I kept my feelings inside. I didn't want to hurt Mom and Dad.

Nicky relayed the information to them. They were disappointed but promised we'd be back the next day. I didn't know how it could be done—coming in sick—but shook my head indicating I would return.

It was a long way back home. Mom and Dad expressed their disappointment. They made me keep promising I would admit myself to the Center. To prove my word I stayed in the apartment all day.

By the following morning, the pain was strong.

"I can't go back there, Mom, without a shot of dope. I don't care what that Cruz guy said!"

We argued.

"No." Dad insisted that Mom not give me any money.

"If you don't give me the money, I'll go and get it some way. I might not come back," I told them firmly.

Mom had seen me in this state many times. She knew I was serious. Finally, Father gave in also and came across with a few dollars. I bought two bags and was immediately back to normal.

As we made our way to Clinton Avenue once again, Mom expressed her fears about my being accepted "high." I assured her everything would be all right—that they would never know.

We arrived in the afternoon. The place was a beehive of activity. Nicky was dressed and preparing to leave the building. He looked at me. "You're high. What did I tell you?"

"Look, man, you said come back and here I am. Isn't that enough to convince you I want to stay?" I pleaded.

He didn't answer but called to the others to hurry up. He said something about going to Pittsburgh, Pennsylvania, to a Kathryn Kuhlman service.

What is he going to do with me? I sat wondering and waiting.

Walking out the door, Nicky stopped and stood over me. Another staff worker encouraged Nicky to accept me. "I'm going to break the rule and let you stay, Victor. I hope you realize what we're doing for you. I hope you're desperate." Patting my shoulder he walked out. I felt a sense of relief.

As he went out the door Nicky called back, "Larry, give this man a bed."

I kissed my parents and said goodbye. I was happy and so were they. As I looked at them and smiled, I realized it had been a long time since any kind of affection had been exchanged between us. For the first time in years, I felt love. At that moment I finally realized how fortunate I was to have parents who cared —and who never gave up on me. My insides melted. I cried as they left.

Larry told me to wait in the lobby while he prepared my bed. He put a Bible in my hand. "Read this, if you like, while I go upstairs," he suggested.

I opened it and looked at the pages. They meant nothing. They were merely words on paper. I was too high to read, let alone understand. I started to nod. Then I fell asleep with my head lying on the pages of God's Word.

"Your bed's ready now," Larry hollered.

I woke up and went to my assigned room. He introduced me to my roommates—Billy "Shotgun" and Philip, the latter being an old-time junkie from Harlem. They had already kicked their habits and were living at the Center.

The only bed left was a top bunk above Philip.

"Give him my lower bunk," Philip told Larry. "He's going to be throwing up—I don't want no showers." He smiled.

"Where's the TV set?" I asked, thinking it would be good to have something to watch and help keep my mind occupied while I kicked my habit cold turkey.

"No such luxury here," Billy "Shotgun" answered laughing.

"You got a nurse here? You know I'm gonna be real sick. I'll need some medication," I informed them as I got under the covers.

"You'll get plenty of medication here, brother. It's called prayer and the Bible. That's all you need. The only doctor we got is one by the name of Jesus Christ." The voice was that of Philip on the upper bunk. "Trust him and he'll do a beautiful job on you. He did for me. I didn't believe in nothin' before I came here. But a miracle happened to me. Believe me—he can do the same for you."

It all sounded familiar, yet foreign. How could God help me? Sure he helped my old lady—but she wasn't a drug addict.

Larry left the room but Billy and Philip continued rapping. They related more details of their experiences with Jesus Christ. They informed me that they were now new Christians. I listened closely but thought, "Was it a game? Were these guys conning the preacher boy Nicky?"

I had figured out who Nicky was and knew of his conversion from the Mau Mau gang in Brooklyn. I had encountered his gang one time when the Roman Lords fought against them. Our gangs were enemies on the streets. He seemed to be for real, but I wasn't sure about these two addicts. Can't trust an addict, I thought, knowing from experience.

Finally, they left me to get some sleep. About one o'clock the freight train (or *fright train,* as we sometimes called it) arrived. It hit me head on. The turkey got cold—real cold. My flesh broke out in polka-dot fashion, like the flesh of a turkey. Then the reaction changed and it seemed as if someone put the turkey in an oven. Cold chills turned to hot ones. I tossed, turned, moaned, groaned, and doubled up in pain. I cursed myself for agreeing to come.

About 3 o'clock Larry came in to check on me. When he saw my condition, he asked my roommates to get up. "Let's go downstairs to the chapel," he suggested.

"What are you going to do?" I asked, staggering down the staircase. My physical shape was in a sorry mess. I was a toothpick in size. I needed a haircut, I looked like "a piece of gum after it had been chewed for a long time," as one addict described it.

Here they were dragging me in my condition down to the chapel. Then they asked me to kneel down so they could pray.

Pray! So this is why they want me here—to pray. And pray they did. They prayed and prayed—and prayed. They each took turns. They prayed so loud I thought to myself, "They must think God is deaf."

I thought he was dead. They prayed, but the more they did the sicker I got.

Larry asked me to pray. "Talk to the Lord," he said almost as a command. "Ask him from your own lips to help you."

I hesitated. I really didn't want to. I started, "God...

Oh God, please...help me. I... please God." The words seemed to fall like icicles. I slumped down on the floor, too drained of strength to raise my voice. They continued praying.

After what seemed to me hours they helped me back upstairs and into bed. I began to think about the door. I was told I could leave whenever I wanted. A pusher, I knew, was within two or three blocks. I toyed with the idea.

Daylight came and with it more relief. Throughout the day I talked again with my roommates and crawled in and out of bed trying to catch a few winks of sleep. When I was up I walked the floor. I even picked up a Bible once and tried to read it. Later in the day, the pains returned. Night came again. Minutes seemed like hours. The bloodstream, if it could have talked, would have screamed, "Do something for me! Fix me up!"

Throughout the second night, I played mental games. I saw myself putting wooden blocks together, one on top of another. I said, "If I can only keep putting them up I can go to sleep!" I did, and for a few minutes I fell asleep— then woke up again and mentally reached up and put another block on the stack. Just when I thought the last block was in place, and sleep would overtake me; a strong wind blew and knocked the blocks. This woke me to the torture of withdrawal. The mental game was symbolic of my life.

I made several trips to the bathroom to throw up. It was mostly blood since I had eaten very little. I put on a coat to relieve the cold chills.

Again this night Larry appeared. He placed a mattress on the floor next to my bed; and after praying and giving me a rub down, he lay down on the mattress. Later the same night Nicky Cruz came back and he prayed for me as well. I couldn't understand why they kept praying so much—especially since I didn't think I was getting any better —and it irritated me at first. But the more I thought about it the more I respected them for giving so much attention to me and my need. I decided they were all right guys.

Then one morning, while it was still early and before the sun came up, I decided to leave the Center. Almost before the thought finished germinating in my mind, there stood Nicky over me ready to pray and preach.

"Victor, your problem is not drugs, or the needle," he began. I was captivated by his words, "Your problem is not drugs. You're a sinner. You need Jesus to forgive your sins and come into your heart and cleanse you completely. You're not a sinner because you shoot dope—you're an addict because you're a sinner first of all. Your sin came first, then your drug habit. Sin is like a cancer. In some people, it breaks out one way—in others another way.

Drugs, in your case, are only the product of sin. It's the fruit on a tree that's corrupt. As soon as you ask Jesus to come into your heart, he'll forgive you of your sin and clean you up inside—then the drugs will automatically disappear."

This time he wasn't really preaching at me, but simply talking softly and warmly. He continued, "This is one thing we can't do for you. We can pray—sure. But until you ask Jesus personally yourself, this cleansing and freedom will not come."

The words sank in for the first time, although not all the way. "I'm not ready for this," I thought to myself. I could not conceive how God could transform a hopelessly bound drug addict.

I went back to bed and rolled over in the covers—hiding myself from the truth. Again, I decided to leave later in the morning. I felt strange about leaving after all they were trying to do for me.

Two hours later I mustered up enough strength to leave. I reasoned things in my mind to justify leaving. One reason was that I hadn't slept in three days. I wasn't able to keep food down was another and my entire body was wracked with pain and my bones were brittle. I also felt that seventy-two hours of suffering was more than anyone can take. All these reasons justified my leaving. Furthermore, even God hadn't done a thing for me like they promised He would. I really did a good job of convincing myself.

Downstairs I rested on the lobby bench, exhausted and weak. The door loomed large before me. Beyond it laid the streets, the subway, my neighborhood—and a delicious bag of dope. I could taste it. The very thought of it gave me new strength. Slowly I made my way to the door—choosing a moment when no one was watching me. I didn't want to hear another sermon or hassle with another minister. I reached the door and put my hand on the knob and turned it. "Victor, Victor," a voice called out behind me.

I turned to see Philip rushing at me. "Wait, man, don't give up so easy. Look, you've been here two, almost three days now."

As he talked, he slowly nudged me back onto the bench. A new face greeted me. I was to learn later it was Don Wilkerson, brother of David Wilkerson, the founder of Teen Challenge. Don was a helper at the Center. He and Philip stood over me like prison guards. I felt that they were purposely trying to prevent me from leaving.

I began to feel strange. My heart pounded. I suddenly began to feel guilty about leaving—guilty even for being a drug addict. I couldn't understand the feeling that came over me. I knew it wasn't withdrawal symptoms.

I thought about God and began weeping. I got up and turned toward the door of the chapel. Inside, I went to the middle of the room and got on my knees. The feeling inside me automatically dictated that I should call on God. Like a magnet, words of prayer were drawn out of me.

I actually sought release through prayer. I screamed out the words in a volcano of emotion, "God! Oh God! If you could change a dirty drug addict like me, I am now asking you to do it. I ask you from the bottom of my heart. Please forgive me—come into my life—make me a new man. Take away this ugly dope habit."

This was it—my moment of encounter. If God was God— if he had power, if he was real—I was giving it all I had by humbling myself before him and throwing myself on his mercy. I instinctively felt the need for God as I intuitively knew that he was my only hope.

My past flashed before me. I saw the pot party when I smoked the first reefer. I saw the mainline drug injections—the crimes I committed—the hospitals, jails—the bad scenes at home, the faces of my family. I cried like a baby at the memory of my sins and miseries. "Don't let me live like an animal anymore. Please, Jesus." I used the name of God's Son for the first time.

"Touch me with your almighty power and make me a new person," I freely said, and as I did, a deep faith flooded me. God was no longer someone afar off, or dead. He was here and now—in the room with me—inside me. The shakes in my body stopped and my hands steadied. I threw them upwards toward heaven and began to thank Jesus for saving me.

Soon the chapel was filled. The noise of my prayers and the vibrations of praise reached the upper floors and others came to get under the same cloud of God's presence. Those who had already experienced what I was at that moment, knew I had "prayed through" to victory.

Forty-five minutes later I was in my room sleeping like a baby. It was the first such rest in over seventy-two hours. Eight hours later I woke up to a new day—and a new life. I did not know the term yet, but I knew I was "born again." The old Victor, the junkie sinner, lay buried in the chapel. The new Victor touched his feet down on the floor, *"shod with the preparation of the gospel of peace."* [1]

After breakfast and food—food that stayed down and tasted like food—Nicky Cruz approached me, "How do you feel, Victor?"

"Like new," I proclaimed as I smiled from ear to ear.

---

1. Ephesians 6:15

# 10

# THE SPIRIT

The following days I slowly regained my health. My taste buds came back to life, and food became enjoyable rather than just endurable.

The best feeling, however, was the freedom from craving drugs. It was gone—completely gone. I knew it had to be God who performed such a miracle. Within a period of twenty-four hours, I had changed from a dope-crazed, animal-like existence, to a living, loving, feeling person.

I became a part of the family of God.

It was now summertime and many Bible school and college students were a part of the street witnessing teams who also lived at the Center. There was, at that time, no special or separate program for the converted addicts and gang members, so we joined them on the streets at the rallies and witnessing ventures. That was a small miracle in itself. I was a fresh new convert from the drug life going out on the very streets, among the very people, that had turned me onto dope—but God protected me.

Another thing God did for me was to take away my cigarette habit. It had become a three to four-pack-a-day habit and it seemed I was hooked more on tobacco than heroin. I was the typical picture of the junkie standing on the street corner nodding under the influence of drugs, who always had a cigarette dangling from his hand. I got all I could out of it, smoking the weed down to the very bottom, much like the marijuana smoker does to get the best at the last. My fingers were yellow and parts of my body marked because of the times I had fallen asleep smoking, only to be awakened by a small, smoldering fire.

God took it all away. My mind was too full of new, exciting, fresh and clean things to puff on a white pacifier.

Since then, I've really been grateful for the victory over the cigarettes, especially when I have watched others struggling to overcome the habit.

I learned quickly that the Christian life is not merely giving up, or quitting certain habits. It is growing, learning, experiencing, feeling, and knowing.

I gained a lot of respect for Nicky Cruz as he helped me in this growing process. He became my model. I recognized him to be a man of God. Nobody in the Center could put anything over on him. In chapel, he told us, "God's angels have a telescope and they're looking at you all the time. You could say they are checking you out. Don't be a phony, and don't try to fool God. You'll end up being the fool." He understood us and that's why his messages got through.

After two weeks at the Center Nicky said to me, "Do you want to get out of the city and go to our special training program in Pennsylvania?" After careful consideration, I felt ready to go.

Mingo, a friend from my neighborhood, was chosen to go at the same time. He too lived on Powell Street. One day when he was looking for me he went to my house and my dad told him what Christ had done for me, and then gave him a gospel tract with the Teen Challenge address. He came for a visit, gave his heart to Christ, and remained in the program.

Together with Mario, Larry, Nicky, and Mingo, we headed for the hills of Pennsylvania through the Holland Tunnel.

As we sped along Route 22, passing scenes totally new but breathtaking to my eyes, we sang a Spanish chorus, "No Hay Dios Tan Grande Come Tu" (There Is No Greater God than Our God). Seeing the beauty and freedom of the countryside made me realize how much I had been a prisoner not only of drugs but also of the asphalt jungle. I knew nothing else. Now God was giving me the opportunity to see his handiwork.

Three hours later we drove up "God's Mountain," the small hill on which the Training Center is located. It was opened in 1962 by David Wilkerson to provide a place for drug addicts who had been reached in the city but needed the peaceful country atmosphere to develop their Christian life.

Inside the Training Center Nicky put me in the hands of a new spiritual father, Reverend Frank Reynolds, director of the Training Center. In the months that followed, I learned to love and respect him in the same manner as I did Nicky. I joined twenty other guys from the city who were at the farm. They, like I, had accepted the Lord.

After being assigned a room and meeting my new roommates, I took a walk, exploring the woods, fields, and barn. I collected my thoughts as I strolled. Things had drastically and dramatically changed in two weeks. Before, I sniffed dope into my nostrils; now, I filled my lungs with pure air. As I made my way to the highest point on the hill and looked out over the green fields, I contrasted it all with Brownsville, Brooklyn, and Powell Street—and I cried for joy.

Chapel became my favorite time of day. But there was plenty of work to do. And, to get an ex-drug addict to work anything other than angles is in itself an act of divine power. I was assigned to work in the barn—with the cows.

My roommate Angel asked me to go with him to the barn for his first assignment. I was assigned to go the following morning. Brother Graybill, the owner of the farm, instructed him about his next chore. "Angel, go pick up that bucket, take the sponge, and wash the cow before we teach you how to milk it," he said.

Angel looked at me, "Milk the cow and wash it—what for?"

"Go ahead, man. What's wrong with you? Do what the man told you," I urged him, very glad it was he and not I doing the job.

He didn't move.

"Go on, what you waiting for? The cow ain't gonna bite you," I said half laughing. I kept after the reluctant city boy turned farmer. With sponge in hand, he began wiping the poor cow's face.

"Why I got to wash the dumb cow's face," he asked, feeling and looking stupid.

With the help of Brother Graybill, he was directed to the proper place to wash the cow and was on his way to becoming a seasoned farmhand. The next day I too joined those ranks.

Each day I learned something new—outside the barn as well as inside. God began moving in my heart, changing my thoughts and giving me a peace I had never experienced before. The more I received, the more I wanted.

During an evening chapel service a visiting speaker, an elderly, white-haired gentleman, spoke about the baptism of the Holy Spirit. I had heard some of the staff and guys speaking in other languages as they prayed and worshiped the Lord. Although I didn't understand it, as he preached, it was made clearer and I became curious. I prayed that it might happen to me. Sometimes I remained in the chapel several hours seeking the Lord to fill me with His Spirit of power and love in a new way. On other occasions, seven or eight of the guys would gather in someone's room to pray late into the night. During one of these times, my friend Mingo received the Holy Spirit. I was both happy and upset about it and asked the Lord, "Why is it that Mingo got saved after me, but received your baptism before me? I deserve it first." This only made me more anxious to receive.

A few weeks later another visiting minister spoke on the same subject. As he preached about "the Pentecostal power, the old-time power, and the fire of Pentecost," I got very excited as he began singing a song about it.

"They were in an upper chamber; they were all with one accord, when the Holy Ghost descended, as was promised by the Lord.... Oh Lord send the power just now.... Oh Lord, send the power just now...and baptize everyone."

By the time he came to the end of the song I felt raised six inches off the pew—and closer to the Lord. The preacher came down off the platform, pointed at me saying, "Brother, you're going to receive the baptism of the Holy Spirit." It was all I needed to release my faith. The stop- per was pulled and the river of living water flowed out of my innermost being. Something came over me. I felt as if I had left the world for a few moments. I knew where I was—and yet I knew I was in touch with another world.

At that moment, I spoke in other tongues.

While I praised Him in this new language, God gave me a vision—whether in my mind or with my eyes I do not know, nor does it matter, for the effect and reality of it was the same. A big cloud came down on a cornfield. An individual was in the middle of the cloud. I could not see the face. People were worshipping the one in the middle. Then I saw the cloud go up to heaven and disappear. I knew I had experienced the nearness of the Lord Jesus like I never had before. While in His presence, I thought, "If this is the joy we get down here on earth when the Spirit makes Jesus real, how much greater will it be in heaven?"

The infilling of the Holy Spirit affected me in various ways. It broke down the fear of speaking out for Christ. It loosed me from psychological bondage. I wasn't afraid to testify or personally speak to individuals about what the Lord had done for me, and what He could do for them.

Brother Reynolds invited me to give my testimony at a high school assembly. Not even the 1,500 faces staring at me could hold me back. There was a burning fire within me. The words flowed as though they were coming from a living fountain inside. And I made the mistake of not shutting off the fountain in time. I began telling the students about the baptism of the Holy Spirit and speaking in other tongues. Brother Reynolds finally pulled my coattail. I felt embarrassed, yet at the same time happy, to tell the whole world, "Jesus is alive!"

I received a call from my parents soon after and explained to them about my baptism in the Holy Spirit. I didn't exalt this experience above salvation; but for a drug addict who has lived on "highs" most of his life, the baptism in the Spirit showed me that one could experience Christ in a dramatic, euphoric, yet glorious, fashion—as well as learning the life of dedication, discipline, and truth.

Since then I have learned that the most important part of being a Christian is in the walk—the life of obedience; of following the teaching of Christ. Yet there are spiritual "highs," as I referred to them. Some Christians feel they don't need the Spirit's infilling, or that it is not the will of God for them, and I respect their opinion. But I thank God first for my salvation and deliverance from sin, which, of course, included drugs. I am also extremely thankful the Spirit saw my inner needs and gave me a demonstration of his power. It was the icing on the cake.

# 11

# TEMPTED AND TRIED

It was time to come down off the mountain. For three months I had been on "God's Mountain" at the Training Center. They were three months of living in a mountaintop experience, spiritually speaking. Now I wanted to visit my people in Brownsville, to try my spiritual wings in the devil's pit. Rev. Reynolds cautioned me, "It would be better to wait, Victor, till you're sure you're ready. Remember, the devil lost a good worker when Jesus found you; he's not going to let you go without a fight."

"I believe I am ready now," I answered assuredly.

"All right, you can go, but make sure you get alone with God and ask for the special 'protecting angels' to accompany you," was his last instruction after granting permission for a weekend pass.

It was springtime. I got off the subway in Brownsville which was like another world to me. Three months ago it was the only life

I knew, but now it was a chapter from the past. As I walked down the main streets, it was a comforting feeling to know there was more to life than the Brooklyn ghetto—and three bags of dope a day. I approached my apartment house with an air of confidence. "Thank God it's only a visit," I said to myself, viewing the typical garbage-strewn streets, the wall-to-wall people, and the familiar mixture of noise and smell. I had nothing to compare with Powell Street and the ghetto before my transformation. Now I knew life could be different and better—I could compare. I decided I liked Pennsylvania, apple pie, and America more.

My daydreaming was interrupted as I spotted Charlie. "Long time no see," I said as we exchanged back slaps.

"How you doin', you look slick, man," Charlie commented looking at my suit and nice shoes. "What happened to you?"

"I'm different, Charlie—no more junk. I'm with God now. Jesus Christ changed my life." I stated. I felt strange at first as I began talking about the Lord to an old friend from the street life for the first time.

He looked at me suspiciously and didn't say anything for a moment. "You got to be kidding, man," he finally laughed. "You know you'd like some stuff. I can't believe what I'm hearing from Victor Torres. Not you, man, anyone but you. I bet you'd shoot up right now if I put some stuff in your hands. Since you been gone there's been some strong junk comin' around here."

"No. I'm clean. I don't need the stuff anymore. I got peace of mind another way." I tried to convince him I was serious and not playing some kind of game.

"Man, why don't you get straight? You know we both can get down on one bag. Believe me, it's good stuff, Victor." The more he spoke the weaker I felt. Yes, I did remember what a fix of heroin felt like. Yes, it was a terrific sensation; I had to admit to myself. Charlie was starting to get to me. Perhaps I was missing something.

As soon as I began to give into such thinking and temptation, the devil rushed in like lightning and said, "Maybe one little shot is not going to kill you. It won't hurt you in the least." Charlie beckoned me to follow him. I trailed along as if in a daze.

"You got bread?" he asked. "Ah, yea... I... got five bucks on me," I responded.

"Well, what we waiting for?" he asked, quickening the pace. A block and a half later we walked into the lobby of a familiar apartment house.

"Gimme the bread," he said. I didn't move.

"Don't worry, Victor, I know how you feel. But one second after the white magic is in you; all those fears and worries will be over." Charlie saw my reluctance and took time to reassure me. He kept on speaking, but I wasn't listening. I thought about what to do to cover up after the shot. How would I hide it from my parents? And if I didn't go home and went back to the Center, there were too many former addicts to face. They would know immediately I'd gotten high. What was I to do?

Then it came. Just like old times. Whenever I needed a scheme to hide the truth, to cover a crime, there seemed to be a super intelligence working in me.

"Take the fix of heroin and sleep it off in some basement. The next morning go home and tell your parents you stayed at the Center. When you get to the Center, tell them you stayed with your folks." It sounded foolproof. No one would ever know. Now all I had to do was give the money to Charlie. But before I could get the money out, the pusher arrived.

"You cats want to score?" He inquired.

"Baby, you're just the man we been wantin' to see," Charlie said as his face lit up at the sight of the man with the bags.

He shook my arm, motioning to get the money. I slipped a hand in the right pocket and felt the five dollar bill.

Touching it I suddenly felt as if something was wrong. My hand froze in the pocket, still holding the money. An inner voice spoke clearly, "No...no, this is wrong. No, Victor, don't buy the drugs. Get out of here right now!"

I immediately recognized the work of the Holy Spirit. Like he had done so many times during the three months of my conversion to Christ, whenever I stepped out of line, the Holy Spirit came to "convict of sin." This time the voice was as sharp and clear as it had ever been. I was reminded of the glorious encounter with Christ on the chapel floor at the Brooklyn Center. The euphoria I experienced with the infilling of the Spirit at the Training Center and the many other blessings of the new life I enjoyed came flooding back. All of it flashed through my mind in a moment of time— while Charlie stood anxiously waiting for the five dollars.

A scripture came to mind, "Whom the Son hath set free is free indeed." As it did I bowed my head and began shaking it back and forth. Then I said out loud, "No ... No, No ... I can't do this. Devil, you're not going to get me. I am free!"

"What's wrong with this guy?" the pusher asked Charlie.

"I'm not sure," Charlie replied. "But he's been a little weird since I met him. He's in some religious place and I think they ate his mind. He ain't normal now."

As the two of them watched I walked out the door and ran toward my house. "Thank you, Jesus," I repeated out loud several times. I came out of the daze and regained my composure. Walking up the stairs to our apartment I raised my head high. I knew I had just experienced the greatest victory of my new but short-lived Christian life. If I had any doubts before regarding the power of God, and His ability to keep me, they were now gone. He had proven himself to me when it counted the most. Right out in the heat of battle, in the face of danger and temptation, the Lord taught me by personal experience that "greater is He that is in you, than He that is in the world." It was to be a lesson I never forgot.

At home, I related to my folks what I had just gone through. We got right down on our knees and had a prayer and praise service. Then we got up to celebrate my newfound cure and the return of the Torres' dead son back to life.

After such an emotional visit I decided not to give further place or opportunity to temptation and the devil by staying in the neighborhood too long. We had been taught that the Lord did not give us *"the spirit of fear, but of power, and of love, and of a sound mind."* [2] But, at the same time, we were to have respect for the powers of evil and not to *"give place to the devil."* [3]

I remembered the teaching and returned to the Center that evening to await the trip back to Pennsylvania to further my Christian development.

The following Monday after getting back to God's Mountain, I felt as though the Lord had helped me pass the first semester's finals. I was ready to go onto bigger and harder lessons.

---

2. 2 Timothy 1:7
3. Ephesians 4:27

# 12

# THE GIRL FROM MEXICO

Victor, how would you like to work for Teen Challenge in Boston this summer?" Dave Wilkerson asked me.

With six months of Christian living behind me, like many newborn and enthusiastic Christians I got the "what-am-I-going-to-do-in-the-future" jitters. So, I told him I would.

I loved the farm and the Training Center, but a strong feeling of "I gotta go" came on me. We were continually cautioned not to "get ahead" of God. We were taught to take heed lest we not finish building the foundation of our Christian walk and go out too soon which could result in our falling back into drugs. I had seen too many do just that during my time in the Center.

I also knew I must avoid getting "hooked" on Teen Challenge. The drug addict (and even the non-addict I have subsequently learned) finds it difficult to make changes. We find security in a place or job and like to stay there— fearful of a new challenge, new faces, new places, and new responsibilities. I sang the words often in the chapel services, "I'll go where you want me to go, dear Lord. I'll do what you want me to do."

Now it was time to put feet to the words. I said goodbye to Brother Reynolds and all the staff and then left for Boston.

The trip took me through New York and I spoke to Nicky.

"I think you ought to go to Bible school," he said. "Davie and I will arrange the money for your tuition. I want you to plan to go this September," he stated as a matter of fact and without asking my opinion. But it was Nicky's way. If he felt something was of God, he didn't beat around the bush. He had learned to lead a gang with authority; and when he felt he had the mind of the Lord, he also led with authority.

"I'm not sure, Nicky. I'll pray about it and let you know," I answered.

"I've already got three hundred dollars for you," he said with his mind already made up regarding my future.

I decided to delay the decision until I'd spent some time working in Boston.

I was glad to get away for the summer and plunge into the work which was just being established. Since the Center was so new, the ministers and other Christian workers involved in it depended much on the converts from the street scene to help in communicating with the drug users. We knew how they thought, what their lifestyles were— and most of all, where to find them. And, we were the best proof of the reality of the gospel.

I enjoyed sharing my faith—and seeing others helped. I felt as though I was "somebody." After years of frustration and failure and being a detriment to society while being a pain to my parents, and a burden to the taxpayer—I could now contribute something not only to the kingdom of God but to society and mankind. It was a small way of paying back to the Lord and others for my past.

After several weeks of witnessing on the streets, testifying in churches to civic clubs, colleges, and on radio and television; I knew Nicky Cruz was right. I must go to Bible school and prepare for the ministry.

I recall what Dave Wilkerson said to a congregation of solid middle-class Christians on one occasion. "If you will not accept the challenge to tell those outside the church what Christ can do, he'll reach into the gutter, the dope den, the hippie pads, and the asphalt jungle to raise up a gang member, dope addict, or prostitute to do the job."

As I ministered on the streets, I realized I was the very fulfillment of that prophecy. I didn't know much about the Bible and my English was poor and unpolished—but there was something real inside me. I didn't have to pump myself up to work or witness for the Lord; it just came out naturally. No one ever had to teach me a special course on soul-winning. The desire was just there, and the ability came as I went into the "highways and byways" telling people about Jesus.

By August, I was ready to go to Bible school. As exciting as the work was during the summer, I was drained spiritually. I also knew I couldn't always get by just giving my story and testimony of deliverance from drugs. I needed to know the Bible; how the plan of salvation was brought down to man, from Genesis to Revelation, and how the church came to birth plus the many other truths. I needed to learn to *rightly divide the word of truth*[4] and to be a *good workman that needeth not to be ashamed.*[5]

While working at the Center, I had the opportunity to accompany the staff on speaking tours in which I gave my testimony.

---

4. 2 Timothy 2:15
5. 2 Timothy 2:15

I recall a service in Fort Wayne, Indiana, in the Gospel Tabernacle, a Christian Missionary Alliance Church. It was a youth service with about eight hundred in attendance.

After the service, I was shaking hands in the back when a man, woman and a young girl approached me.

"Hi, I'm Mrs. Snyder and this is my husband and daughter," the woman spoke first and introduced the family. "We just want to say that we enjoyed your testimony tonight."

I thanked her. The husband then spoke and said, "Praise God, Victor. While you were speaking a thought came to mind. It was about your needs—your personal needs, I mean. You mentioned you were planning to go to Bible school this fall."

"Yes, that's true."

"Well, do you have the money?" he asked. "Yes, for the first year."

"Oh, we just wondered because we were willing to help if you needed it," Mr. Snyder stated.

Immediately I thought of someone else's need —and said, "But you can help my friend back at the Center. He has no help," thinking of Eddie from my old neighborhood.

Their faces lit up at the suggestion. "Yes," they replied, "we'll be more than glad to help your friend. Just have him write us."

I was anxious to get back to the Center and break the good news to Eddie. But before I could find him I was given some bad news. I was informed that Eddie left the program.

"Oh, no," I gasped. I felt a knot of sorrow well up inside. I immediately headed for the neighborhood looking for him where I met a few of the regular neighborhood "junkies," and they told me what I suspected, "he's on the needle."

I wrote the Snyders and told them the sad news. To my surprise they wrote back and said they were willing to pay my second and third year of school.

The blessings I was receiving so early in my Christian walk were more than I could imagine. The Lord had saved me, filled me with his Holy Spirit, enabled me to go in front of large crowds of young people and others to tell of the grace of God, and now He had provided me with three years of Bible training—even before I started school. In addition, He provided in the Snyders, spiritual parents who prayed for and encouraged me. I could hardly ask for more. I sang, "Every day with Jesus is sweeter than the day before."

"California, Here I Come," became the song and prayer of four of us who headed west to La Puente, California, the home of the Latin American Bible Institute where I had been accepted as a first-year student.

After registering and getting settled into a dormitory setting again, we had our first "get acquainted" service. There the first-year students met our Dean of Men, Brother Camarillo. He spoke a few words of greeting and went over some of the rules and regulations. Had I known the number of counseling sessions I would be spending in his office, I would have packed up right then and headed back to New York City.

After the faculty introductions, every student was asked to stand, give his name and quote a Bible verse. The studies were all in Spanish, and as I listened to various students rattle off their scripture verses my heart sunk. My Spanish was the street version—part Spanish, part English, and part neither. The neither came out that night. I was embarrassed and finally ended up giving the verse in English.

The teachers wasted no time in giving us the assignments and homework. I was overwhelmed. Not only were the lessons hard but the discipline was even harder. I felt caged up. Before, I had ruled my own life—at least to a certain extent, apart from drugs. Now I had to submit total authority to God and the faculty. At the Center, it was somewhat the same, but there it was easier because I knew I needed the strictness to protect me from drugs and the old life. But now that I was a "new creature in Christ Jesus," somehow the strictness was more difficult to swallow. And in spite of myself, I learned something about submission, humility and dying to self.

Even though I was handicapped academically, the Holy Spirit opened my mind to learn. Overall, I was able to maintain passing grades. But the rules were still harder to pass than the tests. The hardest rule, I thought, was the one which stated in bold print— NO DATING. Having a girlfriend in any way, shape, or form was strictly taboo. I decided God had called me to the school to change that. I got a group of guys together and made plans to "protest" to the administration.

We were turned down flat. I decided it was impossible to buck this age-old tradition of the school. We had to revert to other means of communicating with the opposite sex. Such things as note passing, eye contact, work assignment contact and using a third party to carry on expressions of romantic interest were necessary. It never ceased to amaze me, with the strict rules and non-dating policy, how many couples did get together and marry in spite of the policy. I learned that love is stronger than Bible school rules.

During my second semester, I was asked to join the choir. This was a surprise since I couldn't carry a tune in a bucket, bathtub, or shower. "Why do they want me in the choir?" I asked myself. It took several weeks to find out. When we went on choir tours, they had me give my testimony and speak. I became the official choir speaker.

"Preach good, but don't sing too loud," the others in the choir always reminded me when heading out to another church for a concert.

I concluded that my first year in Bible school was a success.

The second-year adjustment was much easier. I had come to accept the rules—no dating and all—and my Spanish improved. So did my eyes. One afternoon the Dean of Women came knocking at my door with a student named Carmen. There were only two students that had access to cars—myself and one other guy, Reuben. His car was getting repaired so the Dean said, "Victor, can you take Carmen to San Fernando Valley she left some of her books at home." "I'll pay for the gas if you'll drive."

Carmen wasn't my favorite person on campus. It seemed like every time a professor asked a question she always knew the answer. Without delay I shrugged and said, "No, my car was sick," my eyes not yet focused on her.

I closed the door to my dorm room, then something inside me awoke as I opened the door again. I leaned out the door just in time to see the most beautiful pair of legs walking away.

I thought to myself, "what, are you crazy?" I immediately called out to them and said, "Sister Carmen, (that's how we addressed each other in school) you will never believe this but my car just got better."

"Oh thank you very much. I appreciate this," she said so lightly.

As I drove the car towards the girl's dorm Saturday morning, I wondered if Carmen would have been so nice to me if I hadn't had a car. Regardless, it would be nice to be alone with a girl for a few hours.

I should have known better. As I drove up to the dorm there stood Carmen, along with good old faithful—the Dean of Women! "Wow, this is too much. I'm a second- year student—a Christian brother studying for the ministry—and they don't trust me. I feel like passing them right by."

But I didn't. "Maybe she doesn't trust Carmen," I laughed to myself as our chaperone climbed into the car, perching herself smack in the middle between us. "Boy, she really doesn't take any chances. What does she think I could do with two hands on the wheel? Anyway, I have no real interest in this girl."

A few miles down the road the two passengers broke the silence by singing coritos (short Spanish choruses). Mile after mile they sang as I sat quietly, minding my own business and paying attention to the road. I started thinking, however, about the young lady on the other side of the dean. She was wearing a pretty white dress with red polka dots. I began sneaking little glances at her out of the corner of my eye. After about the sixth peek I had a little conversation with myself. I knew it wouldn't do any good to try and talk to Carmen; the Dean would interrupt me with another song.

"Victor, where have you been all this time, I thought. "That's a gorgeous Mexican girl."

I debated with myself about her, "Should I make a play for her or not?" I had always said I would only go for a true-blue full-fledged Puerto Rican girl. But the sight of the Mexican girl in the front seat slowly but surely broke down my prejudices. By the time we reached her home my mind was made up, "I'm going to make a pitch for her. She's the one I want."

Back at school that evening I made a beeline for Olivia, a close friend of Carmen's.

"Olivia, I've got to talk to you." I blurted out excitedly. "You're a good friend of Carmen, right? Tell me, is anyone going for her?"

She paused and gave me a sheepish grin, "Well, yes, there is a young man in the local church where she attends on Sundays. I know he's after her, but they are not dating or anything like that."

I interrupted, "But there's no one on campus she likes, is there?" "No, not that I know of," Olivia answered. "She's never mentioned, anyone."

"Well, then, the coast is clear. I ain't afraid of that guy in the church. I can easily compete with him." I told Olivia my honest feelings about Carmen, knowing she would be my carrier pigeon back to her.

I couldn't sleep that night. I was hooked—on Carmen.

The next morning was Sunday and I decided on a plan of attack. "I've got to get alone with her. I've got to tell her how I feel." I had never experienced a feeling for anyone like I did about the pretty Mexican. It was like a fever and I knew only Carmen could calm it. "Ready or not, Carmen, here I come." The street life had taught me this: if you want something go after it until you get it. "Carmen, you don't have a chance," I said, confident of my goal.

At breakfast, I began looking for the right approach. "I'll just go up to her in the dining room and tell her."

"No, you might get caught. A faculty member might see you and then you're in trouble." Since the boys sat on one side and the girls another, it would be obvious I was breaking a rule.

After doing my duty I decided to scout her out. I headed out of the building, and suddenly I spotted her in a classroom, sitting alone by the piano. I stopped in my tracks. We had never really spoken before in conversation. I was scared. I had robbed stores, mugged people, been in gang wars—but walking up to a girl I thought I was in love with, was a totally new scene.

Finally getting up my courage I went into the classroom. "Good morning, Sister Bravo, it's nice to see you again. How are you?" I asked.

She looked up startled and said, "Oh, hello. Hi. I'm fine."

She doesn't even remember my name, I thought. We both stood silent. She acted as if we had never met. I decided to use a do-or-die method and tell it like it is.

"I don't know if you noticed, but on that trip to your house, I fell in love with you," I said, feeling like a fool but meaning every word.

Her head was down and she didn't move.

I continued, "What is your reaction to this?"

She gave me a disgusted look and said, "Well I didn't come to Bible school to get a boyfriend. Who do you think I am?"

"I know. I feel the same way you do—or I did feel the same. But I have, to be honest about how I feel."

There was no response.

I went on, "I'm not just asking you to be my pen pal or girlfriend or something like that. I don't go for that. I don't want to waste my time. I want to marry you. I have a calling in my life and I want you to go with me. We can travel the world together. Will you become my partner for life?"

I figured I was in up to my neck so I may as well go for broke.

"No, I'm not interested," she said very coldly. "Will you pray about it?" I asked.

"As far as I'm concerned, there's nothing to pray about."

"Well, we'll see about that," I responded walking out angry and rejected.

Her lack of interest didn't bother me. My mind was made up; "She is the one for me." But she was not convinced. There was no indication on her part that she had gotten the message. She avoided me like a plague.

There were other girls that would have been much easier to convince. I found notes in my Bible from girls asking me if I was interested in them. If I looked too long at a girl I would get a note saying, "Why did you look at me like that—are you interested?"

One persistent gal sent me a note, "It's now or never."

I wrote back an answer, "It's never." I told my roommate, "I'm not interested in just a girl—or any girl—I want the right one for my life and ministry." Then I added, "Carmen's the right one."

Throughout the school year, I kept after her. Finally one morning she said (evidently to get rid of me), "If you go speak to my mother about this and she says yes, then my answer will be yes too."

I reacted negatively to this. I couldn't believe it. People still do that, I thought.

She thought she was on safe ground—that this was a good way out. She figured I probably didn't have the courage to ask her mother and if I did, she would surely say no. I also knew she would tell her mother I had been a drug addict, that I was from New York City, and worse, I was Puerto Rican and not Mexican. She counted on these three things for me to strike out with her mother.

I had to wait till the weekend to get up to bat and talk to Carmen's mother.

Driving down the San Fernando Valley freeway, I rehearsed what I would say. I felt strange having to go through what I considered a strange routine in order to get a yes or no from her. Though I didn't understand the family tradition of courtship and marriage, I respected Carmen even more for it. I found myself falling deeper in love. She was different from all the other girls I knew on the streets. Carmen was a woman, not a "chick," as I referred to those I knew in the past. Furthermore, she was no pushover, and it was a challenge to pursue her.

I drove up Mission Boulevard to the Bravo house, my own personal mission about to finally unfold. I knocked on the door. (Carmen was already home for the summer, having gone ahead of me.) Her brother Alex answered. I was invited in.

"Thank you," I said with a lump in my throat, butterflies in my stomach, and rubber in my legs.

I stood in the middle of the living room looking around. I felt as though I were in the center of a ring. Mrs. Bravo sat on the sofa, with Carmen's sister Graciela nearby.

No one spoke and I felt really self-conscious. Finally, Alex spoke to me and we exchanged greetings and began chatting. I kept waiting for the right moment to speak to Mrs. Bravo, my heart pounding heavier and heavier.

Ultimately, I turned to her, "Mrs. Bravo, I want to ask you something very important."

Carmen had come into the room while Alex and I talked, but now left as she knew why I was there.

The two of us were alone.

"I came, Mrs. Bravo, to ask if Carmen could be my girl—and also my wife." The words came out slowly and nervously.

I had hoped for a quick yes or no. But no such luck. She proceeded to lecture me on the responsibilities of providing for a wife. It was rather a lengthy sermon, and I began getting fidgety.

Then at the end of one of her sentences she said yes. I didn't catch it at first, when suddenly I realized what she had said.

"May I take Carmen for a walk?" I asked, anxious to get out of the house before she changed her mind.

Another lecture followed on the traditions of the family regarding dating. I didn't think she would allow us to go, but she said, "You may have one-half hour together."

The half hour was better than nothing. We started walking around the block. I reached over and took Carmen's hand and held it firmly. We paced along in silence. It was just getting dark outside; the evening air was calm and beautiful. Carmen's hand was warm and tender.

"Carmen, you are special to me," I said, breaking the silence. "I'm so glad your mother said it would be all right for us to be together."

"I'm also glad. I had already begun to fall in love with you, Victor," she answered. It was the first time she had responded in such a way.

We continued walking hand in hand. The sun went down as we walked. We came to a big tree that covered the entire sidewalk like an umbrella. I stopped and pulled Carmen closer, taking her hand and squeezing it hard. We exchanged gazing looks.

I wanted so much to kiss her—the moment seemed right for it—but her mom's lecture still rang in my ears and I resisted. I didn't want to spoil things so early in our now approved courtship and contemplated marriage. But still, I wanted to kiss her. "Do you mind if I kiss you?" I ventured to ask.

She blushed, turned her head away, then looked up. "Yes, Victor, I do mind, she answered. "You see, I was brought up this way. No one has ever kissed me before. In Mexico where I was brought up in the little town of Tangancicuaro, where everybody knows everybody else, they taught me that only when you marry does the boy get to kiss the girl. This is the tradition even in my family."

"But you are in America now, Carmen," I protested.

"No, that's the way it's got to be between you and me," she insisted. "I have learned to love you, but I want to wait for the real assurance of our wedding."

I promised myself I would never ask again.

"We won't be able to tell anyone," I told Carmen after we agreed to go together. But as much as we tried to play it cool, hidden romance could not be kept under wraps. The school super-intendent caught us talking too often and we were warned about it. I was president of the second-year class, which involved various activities that brought me in contact (without a rule infraction) with Carmen.

I made the most of it. After the Christmas holidays, we decided to make our relationship known officially to Brother Bueno, the superintendent. All the students knew—in fact, some students knew or thought they knew certain ones were in love even before the couple knew.

Mr. Bueno gave us his blessing and thereafter we were allowed to date. Dating consisted of one-half hour together once a week in a room next to Brother Bueno. Exactly at the half hour, he knocked on the door and the date was over.

At the end of the school semester, Carmen went home. I wanted to take her on a picnic before heading to the East Coast. Olivia, Carmen's friend, and her boyfriend, Zeeke, were to join us. I asked Carmen's mother for permission. I hated to go through the ceremony of asking because I knew there would be another sermon; but it was the only way I could do it, so the sermon was worth the opportunity of dating.

Because I was leaving for the summer, she consented. She even prepared barbecue chicken for us to take along. I was pleasantly surprised by Mrs. Bravo's cooperation. As we got into the car, I turned to Carmen, "At last we're going to be alone for an entire day."

"I can hardly believe this," she looked at me with a smile of surprise. "I know mother, and this is not like her. Let's hurry before she changes her mind."

I laughed as we drove off. "I still don't understand your family tradition, Carmen. It's really hard on me."

"You must remember, Victor, my mother is from old Mexico. The custom in her hometown is very different. You're lucky we're not dating there. When the boy wants to see his girl, they have a difficult task. They date by the boy going by the girl's house as she stands in the doorway. If the way is clear and no one is watching, he stays on the sidewalk while they talk. If they talk too long it attracts attention, so he passes on and has to come back later to take up the conversation where they left off."

"That's even worse than the Bible school courting," I remarked.

"Listen to this," Carmen continued. "When my mother was a girl, sometimes dating was done in the big plaza in the center of town on Sundays or holidays. The girls would stroll in the center of the plaza square, and the boys would as well, but they would have to be walking in the opposite direction. They were not allowed to walk together or in the same direction. Each time they passed, the boy would have a chance to say a few words to his favorite girl—or girlfriend—or give her flowers. All the time this would be going on, they had to bear in mind that their parents were sitting on the benches watching the whole procession."

"Now I understand better why your mother is so strict," I said. At the same time, I wondered why I had to observe the traditions of old Mexico—in America.

We arrived at the peak of a mountain where the picnic was planned. Olivia and Zeeke took off in one direction, and we were completely alone. It felt so good being in the open—away from school, away from the superintendent, and away from mother from Mexico.

After eating we followed a stream of clear crystal water coming down from the side of the mountain. As we walked Carmen's hand was in mine again. All of a sudden I felt her get tense; her hand was shaking. We found a big rock and sat down facing the stream. She turned to face me and held both of my hands. Then I realized she was blushing and struggling to tell me something.

"What's wrong, Carmen?" I asked sympathetically.

"Victor, I wanted to give you a special surprise goodbye gift, but I didn't know what to give you," she said, looking at me and then turning her head away. "But now I know," she whispered as she turned, pulled me closer and kissed me.

I was speechless.

Looking me straight in the eyes she said, "I want you to know you are the first man ever that touched my lips."

After a long pause and silence, both of us stood there expressing our love for each other through our eyes. We then walked back to our picnic area. As we did, I thought about the kiss and loved Carmen even more. Not just because of the kiss, but because of the meaning it held for her in expressing her love to me, and because of the struggle she went through to give me that special gift.

At the end of the school year, Don Wilkerson invited me to return to New York City to be the Evangelism Director of the Center. The reception from the drug addicts on the streets during our open-air street rallies was about the greatest in the history of the Teen Challenge ministry. As a result, the number of addicts coming to the Center increased. For the first time, some had to be turned down because there was not enough room and beds; and a waiting list had to be established. The number of converts increased as well and the ministry became known in all the major drug areas. I enjoyed preaching on the street and witnessing to the junkies who were desperate for a way out of their misery.

In the middle of the summer, I was ready to return to school, especially to Carmen. I was in financial need so I went to see David Wilkerson. I wanted to tell him about my proposed wedding plans and to share my need of money for a ring and the wedding. As a staff member I made twenty dollars a week, but that was used for personal expenses. Brother Dave said he couldn't help me because the Center was in financial need also. "Just take it easy, Victor," he said. "Don't get excited. Your need will be met." But seeing my anxiety, he opened the Bible and began to pray. Then looking up he said, "Victor, the Lord just spoke to my heart and assured me you'll have a thousand dollars by the time you get to Bible school."

I didn't really believe him and said to myself as I walked out of his office, "Brother Dave is trying to pull my leg. How in the world am I going to get that much money—a thousand dollars?"

I needed money for school books, for graduation expenses, a ring for Carmen—and the wedding.

The summer ended and we headed to California. David Wilkerson lined up a few churches for me to speak in on the West Coast. They received me well and I enjoyed telling them about my experiences with the Lord, both in my life and in what he was doing on the streets of New York City.

When I finished the tour and returned to school, I counted the offerings. They totaled just over one thousand dollars! "Thank you, Jesus!" I shouted. I bought a ring and placed it on Carmen's finger.

We set the wedding date following our final school year and graduation.

From September to June, I was like Jacob because all I did was work, study, and wait for my bride-to-be. I sat in the classrooms thinking about going down the aisle to receive my diploma and officially graduating—and about the other aisle, where Carmen and I would be "joined together in holy matrimony." Needless to say, it was the longest year of the three.

The wedding took place on June 17. We spent three days on our honeymoon, and then we headed back to New York where I again resumed the duties of Evangelism Director of the Center. I was back doing what I loved and wanted most—preaching to my people, the drug addicts.

# 13

# CHRIST CONQUERS COMMUNISM

We stood in our "honeymoon" apartment, replete with dirty floors, walls that badly needed painting with used and misused furniture. It was not a sight for starry-eyed newlyweds. We had thought we would get one of the regular apartments for married couples supplied by the Center but instead were presented with a basement apartment, complete with wall-to-wall dirt. We were told we would have to "fix it up."

Having no choice in the matter I painted (spread would be a better description) the walls and Carmen scrubbed and cleaned. When it looked partly livable we started moving the bits of furniture into place. While moving a big, ancient bed, Carmen hurt her back so severely I had to carry her in my arms.

For two months the back pain persisted. In addition, she became ill and when I would come back from street evangelism, I'd take care of her.

Carmen did get better but our ministry got worse. The mood on the streets had changed and the ghetto community was angry. Passivity had changed into militancy so oftentimes, street evangelism met with resistance. There was a spirit of hostility, hate, and evil in the air.

One night while I was preaching, on a street corner, I was hit on the head with a beer can that was thrown from a rooftop. On still another occasion, an egg splattered my suit. Once, a Black Muslim snatched a Bible from my hand and said, "Stop preaching about a white God to these people!"

Rooftops were filled with gangs ready to throw bricks and bombs on the police—and us. Only by invoking the name of Jesus were we spared in certain situations.

While working at the Center, Carmen and I became burdened for South America (a vision we had shared and carried since our courtship). We heard through various sources of the need for a Spanish-speaking American evangelist.

With no pledged financial support, no sponsorship from a mission board or society, and with no invitations to speak or direct contact with anyone in South America—we decided to go.

I spoke in a few churches and raised enough money for our airfare to Argentina, where we both felt the Lord leading us. On a wing and a prayer, we flew the friendly skies to an uncertain land.

"All we have, Carmen, is our vision," I told her. We knew no one in Argentina, had no prearrangements to meet anyone and had no meetings scheduled. However, one day before our flight we were introduced to a Christian sister who gave us the address of her mother who lives in Buenos Aires, with the suggestion we "look her up."

"At least we have one address," I said to Carmen as we sat 35,000 feet in the air speeding along on a mission for souls. This was a complete step of faith and bravery I told myself when moments of doubt arose.

As I looked at Carmen her expression seemed to say, "Are we doing the right thing? Was it the Lord who spoke to us? Are we running away from something?"

We committed our fears to the Lord and left the rest behind.

Eight hours later the wheels of the 707 touched down in Buenos Aires.

"Where's our welcoming party?" Carmen teased.

"Let's try the address we got yesterday," I suggested. We were tired, somewhat bewildered, and starkly alone in a big city.

The taxi took us for two rides: one over the roads to the Christian lady's address, the other over our pocketbook as the driver overcharged us to the tune of ten dollars.

"Just like the New York City cabbies," we both agreed.

The woman welcomed us cordially, for which we were grateful, considering our unannounced arrival with baggage and all. After sharing our mission with her, she agreed to let us stay in her apartment. We were grateful.

"Lord, you found us a bed to sleep on; now find me the place where you want us to preach," I prayed that night. The devil again spoke, "You're a fool. You traveled all this way without, enough money, without meetings. It's all going to be for nothing."

After prayer, my faith increased and I put the devil back in his place.

I began making phone calls to pastors, alerting them of my services and mission. Rev. Daniel Grazo, a leader of one of the Christian movements, was one brother I found with an open mind and heart for the vision the Lord had laid on my heart. We arranged to meet, prayed about some evangelistic endeavors, and within a few days, the wheels were rolling with plans for street rallies, church meetings, and crusades.

The Lord anointed my ministry as I proclaimed the Word of God and shared my deliverance from drugs. In a short time, one door after another opened. One door led to another, and I stepped in as fast as they opened. A sense of satisfaction—and relief—came upon me as I was assured from these openings that the Lord was in our coming.

Souls were saved on the streets as well as in the churches.

I began praying, "Lord, use me in a special way down here! I believe you sent me to South America to do a work for you that others cannot do." I was thrilled with the church meetings—and the street evangelism crusade. But I knew in my heart that there was a special door waiting to open for us.

This knowing became a reality when I began hearing of the need among students in the universities. We received an invitation from Chile to speak at the University of Santiago De Chile. As soon as it came I knew this was the special opening we were sent to undertake. We flew to Chile as soon as possible.

A young Christian student obtained permission from the president of the University for me to speak in one of the school's largest classrooms. He predicted, "I doubt if you'll get anyone to come to such a meeting because these students are all communists."

We visited the school a day before the scheduled meeting and saw why the president made such a prediction. The walls carried large bold letters: "VIVA FIDEL CASTRO, VIVA CUBA, VIVA COMUNISMO."

I got excited seeing the signs. "This is right where we belong," I told Carmen. "This is one of South America's most neglected mission fields."

The next day we arrived—nine Christian students, Carmen, and me—on a campus of several thousand students, mostly communist. We arrived to learn that the communists had scheduled a meeting at the exact time as ours. "Lord, don't let them get the victory," I breathed in prayer. I felt confident of the Lord's presence as we walked across the grounds of the campus to the classroom. We walked up the stairs to the second-floor room—and to our surprise, the place was jammed. About 500 were inside and another hundred outside who couldn't get in.

The professor introduced me and I began by telling of my involvement in narcotics. I then went through the details of my efforts to reform, of the time spent in institutions, in jails, and in hospitals. They listened attentively.

At the right moment, I then shared my experience of encountering the reality of Jesus Christ. The words rolled off my lips with force. I knew the words were not falling flat on the floor, but rather into the hearts of the students. I sensed a deep searching and hunger in many. The atmosphere became charged with the presence of the Lord and the power of the Holy Spirit. The entire room was silent except for my voice.

When I finished no one moved. They then broke out in applause. The professor dismissed them, but many rushed forward to ask questions. The professor came over and said, "Mr. Torres, I would like to arrange for you to come back again. The next time I want the entire medical faculty and students to hear you."

We spent the rest of the day witnessing and praying for students who wanted to receive Christ.

I returned a few days later to see a room full of white-garmented medical students waiting to hear me speak. Once again I shared the testimony of how, in Christ, *old things passed away, behold, all things become new.*[6]

---

6. 2 Corinthians 5:17

In the middle of my story, I said, "Medical science failed to provide an answer to my problem." Suddenly a student in the back of the room stood up and interrupted me.

"Pardon me, Mr. Torres," he shouted. "Science and medicine may have failed in America, but it has not failed here."

Then he asked a very technical question that I could not understand, partly because of my inability to comprehend medical terms in Spanish and partly because of my ignorance of the point he was trying to make. I did understand, however, that he was challenging my testimony—and the power of God.

I was frustrated. I wasn't used to being rebutted in a public meeting, although I was accustomed to it on the streets when witnessing. I lost my train of thought and stood silent. The students sat watching and waiting for my response.

I bowed my head, praying silently. Looking up, I slowly began speaking again—not answering the question directly, but continuing to share what Christ had done for me and in me. My speech picked up momentum. I felt liberty to speak with force and conviction. I was conscious in an unusual way that the Spirit of God had taken over and was speaking through me. I felt as if I had become another person for that moment—and was standing outside of myself, listening to myself. The words, like arrows, were hitting their targets—the minds and hearts of the students.

Then I finished—or the Holy Spirit speaking through me finished. For a few seconds, there was complete silence in the room. Then the entire group, except for the one who asked the question, stood to their feet and applauded. Several turned around waving their hands in disgust at the challenger. "You're wrong," one of them said.

I learned later the point the questioner raised was to deny the miraculous. The Lord had used me as an example to defeat his skepticism and to prove once again that a man with an experience is never at a disadvantage with a man who only has an argument.

We continued our journey going on to Venezuela, Colombia, and Ecuador—again seeing unusual doors of ministry opening to us. The greatest opening was Quito, Ecuador. We had been invited there by Mike Santiago, a young man and his wife and three children; who were already engaged in missionary work.

Mike picked us up at the airport. "Glad you came, Victor. The need is great," he said. He continued by explaining that the country was open to the gospel, but the communists were also doing their thing. As he talked, my heart was burning inside. I listened and looked out the windows of the car as he drove along the crowded streets of Quito.

Then he turned and said, "Tomorrow we start the big campaign in our church. The place where we are going to have the meeting used to be a bread factory. Now we bake the Bread of Life. It is our church."

We started our meeting with the place filled every night. People came from all over the city to listen to the Word of God. Then one night after the service, Mike suggested, "Victor, I forgot to tell you that in Quito there is a university with thirteen thousand students. It has never been touched with the gospel. Maybe during the daytime, we could go."

The idea sank deep into my heart, and it bore witness with Carmen and me.

"One thing Victor, it has more communists than anything else."

As soon as he said that, I remembered the time in Chile. I responded, "Yes, let's go."

I later found out it was about ninety-five percent communist.

The following day, we organized a group from the church and headed for the university. Getting out of the car, I noticed a big red flag in the middle of the campus, with a big stone grave. "That flag, Mike, looks like a communist flag," I said.

"That's right, Victor," he said. "There's another thing, the grave. That's where one of the communist leaders is buried."

We began our talk with some of the students. It resembled very much the university in Chile; only here hearts were much more hardened. A group of students were wearing buttons saying, "I am a communist." I opened my Bible and started to preach to them. They stopped to listen. After a few minutes, a crowd gathered and surrounded us.

"Give me that Bible!" One of the men reached out and grabbed the Bible from my hands. "You are preaching capitalism!" he said, in a loud, angry voice. He caught the attention of others.

Suddenly, I received courage from above. I stood and stretched out my hand and took the Bible out of his hands. "No," I said. "You are wrong, we are not preaching capitalism. I am preaching the Gospel of Christ, and the Gospel is not from America, but from God to everybody in the universe. This is not an American message."

The more I spoke, the more confidence and authority I felt. "I come to bring you a message of love."

They listened and I sensed they respected my boldness.

After we broke up I got an idea. "Hey, Mike! Has anyone ever preached inside the auditorium of the university?"

"No! Never," he responded. "You're kidding me, right? Six months ago there was a revolution. You see those walls with all the bullet holes?"

"Wow!" I said. "Man, these people don't play around." "That's right!" he replied.

"Listen, Mike, I said. "How about trying to get permission from the Director? Maybe we could have a Jesus rally inside."

"Let's try it," he said excitedly.

Mike and I started out toward the office of the Director. Walking down the corridors and hallways, we saw signs all over the place: "Down with Christianity. Up with Communism, Viva Comunismo!" For a moment we felt like giving up. But we continued forward.

Arriving at the main office, Mike asked for the Director. The young lady at the desk answered, "He is not here." Seeing the Bibles in our hands, she suggested that we talk to Herman, across from her.

"I am the Assistant Director. The Director is not here today," he said.

From a room in the back of the big offices, a well-dressed middle-aged man stepped out. "What can I do for you?" he said. "I am the Director."

I said, "We want to ask a big favor."

He very cordially asked us to come in. As we sat down in his office he asked, "What favor is it you desire?"

I started out by telling him who I was and where I came from. I shared a little of my experience with God, keeping in mind that Mike had told me that most, if not all, of the staff, were communist. He stared at us, his eyes falling on the Bible I was holding in my left hand. I continued about how Jesus Christ had changed my life. I noticed that his eyes had a few tears in them. I told him I wanted to share this with the student body. He stood up and said, "It would be a pleasure."

Mike and I turned and looked at each other with great surprise. The Director then asked if we would like to use the theater.

"Yes," I said.

We could not fully believe what was happening. He called his secretary, his assistant, and the man in charge of the theater. He spoke to them with enthusiasm. "Give these two men what they need. They have a message we all need to hear."

We agreed to have a meeting on Monday morning, in the university theater. The theater had a capacity for three thousand people.

"Thank you, sir, very much."

Mike and I walked out with our Bibles and down the stairs to take the good news to the rest of the group waiting for our return.

Mike said, "Victor, this is history for Quito, Ecuador. It has never been done before."

"Praise God," was all I could say. The excitement was overwhelming and the news spread all over Quito to other Christians and churches. We prayed and prepared ourselves. We printed posters for the university walls. None of us knew what the result would be. All I could think about was the three-thousand-seat auditorium, and if it would be full.

The day came. Mike and his wife and Carmen and I took off for the big theater. We arrived early and the place was empty. We could have heard a pin drop. The moment came. The doors were opened, and fifteen minutes before time to start, we had to close them again. Every seat was filled. The air was filled with a spirit of curiosity. Mike stood up and began the meeting and then introduced me. I shared the love of God from the Word, and how it had affected my own life. Questions popped up, one after another, but the results were beautiful.

After I finished, we dismissed the crowd and asked if any wanted to know more about God. If so, would they please come forward, and we would talk to them. About one hundred young people responded and filled the platform where Mike and I were standing. For several hours we counseled and prayed with students.

When the meeting was over, we started walking toward the outside exit. As we walked, the director stood in front of us. He shook my hand and with a strong squeeze remarked, "Mr. Torres that was great. I want you to know that the doors of this university are always open for you to return, anytime. Thank you for the talk."

Shortly after this, word from my parents forced us back to New York.

We returned to find my family in a state of fear. Our neighborhood had grown worse with muggings, robberies, and riots forcing them to remain in the apartment after dark. Even in the daytime, they were fearful of venturing out. They were no longer able to attend church as usual and had become virtual prisoners in their own home.

We had a family conference and decided it was time for them to go back to Puerto Rico and live. I helped make the necessary arrangements and closed up the apartment, severing our last ties with Brownsville and Powell Street.

As we left the neighborhood for the last time, no tears were shed. Life in the apartment at Powell Street had been like a nightmare for all of us. Only by the grace of God and the prayers of my mother had I survived.

Carmen and I put our family on the plane and then returned to the Teen Challenge Center to await the Lord's next move for us.

# 14

## FROM POWELL STREET TO POWELL ROAD

We returned from South America to find ourselves in a familiar position. "Have Bible will preach," was my calling card, but once again the questions were, Where? How? When?

I lined up a few meetings in Richmond Virginia, Memphis Tennessee, and Dallas, Texas; with the intention of ending up on the West Coast.

We packed our bags in Brooklyn while staying temporarily at the Teen Challenge Center. A friend who worked at the Center asked, "Where you headed this time, Victor?" in a tone that seemed to infer I was always heading "somewhere." I stared at him with a blank look on my face and mumbled words to the effect that we were going to California.

Once again we rolled along the open highway. Carmen and I had been married for four years, and the most time we spent in one place was six months. Our car had become our home. Every night or every week it was another town, another state, another meeting, another bed. I accepted it, but I sensed Carmen was weary, although she didn't complain.

As I sat behind the wheel I asked myself and the Lord, "When is this running around going to stop? How long do I have to serve you without financial security, without a permanent home to return to after our meetings?" No answers were dropped into my heart.

Our first stop on the West Coast journey was Richmond, Virginia. Dr. Bob Rhoden, Pastor of the Assembly of God Church, received us warmly. After exchanging greetings I asked him, "May I use your phone to confirm our next meetings?"

Carmen listened as I spoke to the pastor in Memphis, "Yes, I understand. Thank you, anyway; maybe some other time when we're in your area. We'll make other arrangements."

I put down the phone and slowly dialed the operator again. "I'll try Texas now," I said to a worried looking Carmen.

She listened as I spoke to the party on the other end, "Yes, I understand. Thank you, anyway. We'll make other arrangements."

"That's two down, Carmen. I've got a funny feeling we better not try California. I think the door is going to be closed there too," I said as I slumped down in the chair.

"Maybe the Lord is trying to tell us something," Carmen said, not helping the situation as far as I was concerned.

"We're going back to New York as soon as these meetings in Richmond are over," I informed her.

Dr. Rhoden saw our dilemma and suggested, "Victor, why don't you stay right here in Richmond? You could make this your headquarters."

I gave him a negative look.

He continued, "You need to start thinking about your family. You could settle down right here."

I sat silent. "You're out of your mind," I said to myself, upset inside at the mere mention of such an idea.

I looked at Carmen and her face lit up like a Christmas tree. "Victor, I think we should pray about this. It might be a good thing."

"Let's go," I said without answering. We returned to where we were staying. I lay down on the bed and contemplated the situation. I didn't want to pray about it, but said to the Lord, "I don't like Richmond. I feel no call here."

That night we discussed the matter late into the night. Carmen said, "Let's pray," and I kept talking—afraid to pray, for fear of what the Lord might put in my heart.

After exhausting all reasons why we should not stay, there was nothing left to do but pray.

The Holy Spirit spoke through my thoughts, "If I have closed doors, it is for a reason." But the reason was not made known. I knew it would only come by trust and a walk of faith. I had learned that the Lord's will is revealed step-by-step.

The next morning I said to Pastor Rhoden, "We'll give it a try and stay here."

He took me apartment hunting, and much to my disappointment, but to Carmen's joy, the first one was nice and vacant.

"One hundred and fifty dollars a month and you pay the utilities," we were told.

An hour later I signed the lease, paid the first month's rent—and was broke.

"I hope we don't end up in jail, Carmen. I think we made a mistake," I told her as we walked through the empty rooms. "How are we going to furnish this place? We have no money—and no credit." I was disturbed that she didn't seem to be worrying.

Carmen turned to me and said very confidently, "Honey, if this is God's will for us to be here in Richmond, the Lord is going to give us furniture for this apartment."

Then she suggested, "Call Brother Rhoden and ask him about it." I did and he suggested, "Go see Ed Williams in Alexandria. Maybe he'll give you credit."

Ed Williams was a brother in Christ we had met at one of our meetings. He told us about his furniture business. But we had just met him two days before we signed the lease.

We hardly knew him but went to him in faith. Inside the furniture store, our eyes lit up. We had never owned anything in the four years of our marriage. Ed Williams introduced himself again with, "Praise the Lord, brother." A big smile covered his face. I explained our situation.

He listened and then said, "Brother Victor, I'm going to give you open credit to get all the things you need. I'll give you the furniture for the same price it cost me—and I won't charge you interest."

Then he added, "I'm doing this because I have felt from the Lord to help you. I want you to know," he continued, "I am very happy God has sent you to Richmond. Your ministry is needed here. I am not doing this for you but as unto the Lord."

I could hardly believe my ears—and eyes. At first, I didn't want to believe it. I even hoped he would turn us down, so I could finally convince Carmen we were making a mistake by staying in Richmond. But Ed Williams took away my last chance of convincing her.

We walked out of his store with an order of seven hundred fifty dollars' worth of furniture—and seven hundred fifty dollars' worth of bills; to be eventually delivered as well. Carmen thought about the furniture; I thought about the bills. She got the better of the deal.

The following weeks went by slowly. They were the most difficult I had experienced as a Christian and in the ministry. I spoke in a few churches and the rest of the time spent in our apartment pacing the floor. I put a map of the United States on our bedroom wall and looked at it from time to time—picking out all the "other" places I'd rather have been.

Carmen was happy—but I wasn't. I also felt the pressure of the finances. In addition, Carmen informed me we were to have our second child.

By the third month in Richmond I was at my wit's end, ready to run somewhere—anywhere. I was unsettled, miserable, and spiritually low. "I just can't live in this city. It's too small—and it's a hick town," I said. I compared it to New York and Los Angeles and felt lost in it. "Nothing but trees," I said to myself as I wanted to catch the next plane out.

I turned to Carmen finally and said, "Honey, maybe we don't feel peace because we are not in the will of the Lord."

"Well, I don't know about that. I like it here." The assurance of God's will was her answer.

One day in desperation, I called Don Wilkerson. "I think the Lord wants me to go back to New York and work, Don," I said convincingly. He was willing to help and said there was an empty apartment on Long Island where we could stay.

I called a U-Haul truck station and found out the prices and scheduled a date to move our furniture.

A week before the date to leave I decided to call Don again and confirm everything. "Victor, I'm very sorry but I was mistaken about that apartment. It's not empty. You won't be able to use it."

Bang! Another door closed right in my face. "Lord, what are you doing to me?" I complained. Carmen and I got down on our knees and wept before the Lord. I felt somewhat better following our prayers but still did not feel peace in my soul.

I decided to give the streets of Richmond a try and began going out to witness. To my surprise, I began to see a familiar sight—drug addicts and junkies. "Wow, right here in Richmond." I shared my exciting discovery with Carmen.

For nights I walked, witnessed, and introduced myself on the streets. I gave my testimony and passed out literature. I was pleased with the addicts' openness. I told a few to call me at home if I could help—and the phone started ringing. Some were on heroin, some on speed, others just mixed up kids that needed guidance.

Late one night I returned home after a fruitful evening of making good contacts. I picked up the Time magazine, which covered the story of the Jesus Revolution. As I read the report, I recalled that three years previously Dave Wilkerson had predicted the United States would see a great spiritual awakening among youth. "This is that," I said, my heart warming. "This can happen here in Richmond," I felt the Spirit of God impress upon my heart.

I thought of the many I had spoken to on the streets. A sense of compassion and love filled me on their behalf. I placed the magazine on the floor, stretched my arms toward heaven, and called on the name of the Lord, "Oh God, make me a part of the Jesus Revolution." It seemed as though my heart would walk right out of my chest— and head to downtown Richmond to pour the love of Jesus over the heads and lives of the kids on the street.

I woke up the next day with a new attitude toward our ministry—and toward the city of Richmond. I saw the place as a wheat field waiting to be harvested and gathered in. I told the Lord I wanted to be part of the gathering in force.

I soon located a group of Jesus kids out witnessing and went with them to the parks, on the university grounds, the hangouts, and wherever there were groups of kids.

Driving back home from the center of the city one day, I spotted an empty house with a sign outside: FOR SALE.

I had begun to realize the need for a place to house and to help some of those to whom we witnessed. The thought of my opening a place grew stronger every day—and the sight of the for-sale sign struck a note of interest.

I called the broker and was told the price was $17,000. I thanked him and decided to drop the idea. I wasn't ready to try my credit on him.

Two weeks later, passing the same house, I noticed another sign: FOR RENT. I called again and was told they wanted $150 a month.

"I believe we can get that house," I told Carmen as I shared my vision with her.

"We have a three-day Jesus Rally coming up at Rev. Johnson's church.

I'm going to present the challenge there and see what happens." I did just that and two days following the weekend meeting, Pastor Johnson presented me with a check for $500.

"Praise God, Carmen, we're in business! I'm going to call it the Jesus House," I told her.

There were no definite candidates for living at the house, but I knew that by the time we got the place fixed up a little, they would be there. We did, however, have residents already in the house when we got there—rats. "They're so big that if you had a saddle I think you could ride on them," I kidded Carmen after signing the lease.

I rounded up some Jesus kids from the city and we went to work painting and cleaning up the place. As we worked, I began getting advice on how to begin the ministry. Some encouraged me, others discouraged me. What about a permit from the city to operate? Are you sure the neighborhood will accept you? Shouldn't you put an ad in the newspaper before moving in?

Something inside me said, "No, go in and possess the land. Open first and answer questions later."

One day I came into the house to find a young man sitting on a broken down chair in the living room.

"Hi. My name's Forrest," he said, introducing himself from under an unruly mop of hair.

"What can I do for you, Forrest?" I asked.

"I came here to stay," he said in a matter of fact tone.

"Tell me about yourself," I continued as I gathered some paint cans together.

For the next thirty minutes, he shared a story that was all too familiar. A broken home from divorce—dropped out of school— messed up on drugs—in jail—finally in a mental hospital. He had escaped from the mental hospital and the police were now looking for him.

"How old are you?" I asked.

"Fourteen," he answered. I looked at him, noting he was either lying or big for his age. I decided to accept the second explanation as there seemed to be a note of sincerity in his story.

He explained that he came to Richmond where he ran into some Jesus converts. They led him to the Lord and told him about the Jesus House.

"So here I am."

"Well, we're not ready to open yet, Forrest, but you can come home and stay with my wife and me until we are open. It will be a little tight. I have a child and there are two guys, Flip and James, staying with me who are helping here in the house," I explained.

A few days later I called his mother and related the situation. I told her I wanted to help her son, with the help of God.

"Please don't call the police," I said before hanging up the phone. She promised she would not.

A few hours later Forrest's father called from Washington, D.C., and wanted to know all the details. I shared with him how Christ was changing his son's life. "Would you give us and the Lord a chance and the opportunity to help Forrest?" I asked.

Several days later in my house, Forrest was sitting on the sofa reading the Bible. I looked at him and contemplated as to whether I should tell him the news I had learned the day before. We had come home the previous day from baptizing Forrest in water when the neighbor called me over and informed me the police had been to my house.

"They surrounded your place; there were six patrol cars in all," he said with suspicion. "What were they looking for?"

I didn't say but I knew. They were after Forrest. I didn't tell the neighbor because I was already worried as to what they were thinking about me. They knew I was one who kept a bunch of hippies in my house all the time.

There was no time to worry about that now. A car pulled up, along with a police vehicle. Forrest was still reading the Bible. I decided it was time to inform him.

"They're here, Forrest. The police have come. Someone told them where you are," I said. "But don't worry; you're in Jesus' hands now."

He looked up calmly and smiled. "You better believe it. Sure thing, I'm all right. I'll be OK."

The police wasted no time coming to the point and getting their hands on Forrest. He offered no resistance and conducted himself like a gentleman. He began telling them about Jesus but they paid no attention. They led him out the door.

"Victor, I'll see you, man. I've got Jesus with me," he hollered as they put him in the backseat of the police car.

They sped away leaving me with a broken heart, and with my first resident taken out from under me. I prayed silently that the Lord would bring him back.

Since I had no idea where they were taking him, I could not make contact for days. His parents could not locate him either. So I worked in the Jesus House and waited.

Days passed and still there was no word from or about Forrest.

The phone rang one afternoon and the caller informed me she was calling from juvenile court where Forrest had gone for arraignment. She explained that my name had come up in the courtroom.

"Mr. Torres, this boy just stood up on his feet and testified to the judge and court what he felt in his life since Jesus Christ changed him." She told me the whole story.

"May I say something?" I finally interrupted. "Yes, what is it?" she asked.

"Praise God," I hollered into the phone. "What's that?"

"I hope you will understand, ma'am, just what this means to me," I said with excitement.

"No, I guess I really don't, but praise God anyway," she laughed.

"What will happen to him now?"

"The judge has sent him back for more observation. His parents think he is crazy. But I believe the judge is on the boy's side. He will come back to court later," she explained.

She gave me the address of the hospital and I made arrangements to go see him. But they denied me entrance, stating he was in isolation under special care. I got in touch with Forrest's father who in turn finally secured the necessary permission for me to see him.

Fourteen days following his re-arrest I walked into the hospital ward. He was put in with older men, in a small room. Bars covered the windows and door. As I walked toward his room, I wondered where justice, wisdom, and mercy were in putting a boy in such an environment.

Forrest smiled broadly when he saw me. "Oh Victor, it's sure good to see you. This place is out of sight, man."

"How are you getting along?" I asked although I could see for myself.

"These people are nuts," he said. "And I mean the ones that run the place. I had two Bibles when I walked into the place and they've taken them away."

We sat down and talked. He wanted to tell me about the court scene. "Listen to this, man," he said in terminology reflective of the only lifestyle he knew. "In court, I testified about what Jesus did in my life. They think I'm on another trip, so they put me in here. When I got here they made me go to one of those therapy encounter sessions. Everybody started hollering at me. They said, "Jesus Freak! Jesus Freak!"

He paused and put his head down. "Victor, I feel like I have lost my joy."

I let him pour out his feelings. Then we prayed.

"I feel better now," he said after we finished.

We shook hands and as I went out, he looked at me with his usual smile. "I feel the touch of God again."

Two weeks later Forrest was scheduled to appear in court again for the final disposition on his case. Meanwhile, I worked on the Jesus House, setting it up and putting together a legal religious corporation to carry on our ministry. After praying about various names to call it, I felt most comfortable about the name, New Life for Youth. A lawyer drew up the necessary papers and we were in business.

The two weeks passed quickly and I went to court. The judge asked Forrest, "Do you want to return to this New Life for Youth house with Mr. Torres?"

"Yes, sir, I do," he answered.

After hearing the hospital's evaluation—that they could not work with him—the judge looked at Forrest.

"I'm going to permit you to go with Mr. Torres. Apparently, this Jesus' experience has done more for you than all the other places. I am therefore going to release you to the New Life for Youth house."

We left the courthouse rejoicing in the Lord. Forrest's parents, who were skeptical about his so-called Jesus' experience, were also happy, though not yet totally convinced.

As I drove back to Richmond, I silently praised the Lord for allowing Forrest to be released to our Jesus house in such a manner. It was an added confirmation in my heart that the ministry the Spirit was directing us into was his will. I felt that Forrest was the "first fruit" of our labor, and blessings and victories would follow. I felt that all that had happened in and through me was to bring me to this very point in my life—to reach out to fourteen-year-olds like Forrest; to take them by the hand and tell them to "put their hand in the hand of the man from Galilee." I could not remember a moment—except for my own encounter with Christ—when I had felt any happier or "higher."

With the case settled, there was time to finish fixing up the house. The changes going on in the house seem to parallel the continual changes within Forrest as he matured in Christ.

Other guys and girls began coming for help and, soon every bed was taken. The ministry grew slowly—but continually. We began a daily and weekly program of chapel services, Bible study, prayer, witnessing, and work. Saturday night "Jesus Rallies" began attracting Jesus kids, church youth, and others interested in our ministry and a deeper spiritual life.

Additional help was needed and the Lord sent us, a couple with a famous name but a humble spirit—Dwight and Brenda Moody from a local church. "It has to be the Lord, Carmen," I told her when breaking the good news that the Moody's were joining our staff. I continued, "We can't promise them anything except what is found in their own faith."

Faith and dedication it had to be, especially on the salary we were able to pay them—ten dollars a week between the two. Dwight had left his good paying job, and so had Brenda, his wife, who was a secretary; to come and move into a room eight-by-eight. The Moody's, along with Brenda Nash, another young lady on our staff who did counseling, secretarial work and a multitude of other odd tasks; comprised our staff. She, too, was on the ten-dollar-per-week salary. However, it was to be paid only when we had it.

And we did run out of money—often. We also ran out of food. Early one morning Dwight came to me, "Victor, is there enough money in our checking account for bread?"

"We have three dollars," I answered, "and the rent is due."

We just looked at each other and I decided, "These three dollars won't pay the rent, so use it for food."

I went to my office to get the checkbook when a car pulled up to the house. I stopped to see who it might be and two ladies got out. They walked up the front path with a brown bag under each of their arms.

Dwight greeted them and was handed the two bags. "Wow! Look at this," he hollered with joy; "Groceries!"

He took the bags and set them down. I hurried out as we looked at the contents. I happily shouted, "Three loaves of bread and some sweet cakes. Praise the Lord!"

We thanked the ladies and they went on their way.

To us they were angels. Heaven had seen our need and performed what we considered to be a simple but nevertheless real miracle.

Our family needed miracles as well. I was not on salary. Everything that came in financially went to the Center. When I didn't know where the next fifteen or twenty dollars were coming from, for food and other necessities, I would look at Feliza and Rosalinda, my two children, and desperately ask the Lord to help me properly provide for them. Invariably an invitation to speak would come and with it a small offering to tide us over, or someone would mail a check or give us a donation.

Coming home from church one Sunday afternoon, knowing there was almost nothing in the cupboards to prepare a nourishing meal, we came upon a box at our doorstep as we went inside. It was a box packed full of groceries. Carmen and I looked at each other, not really surprised but grateful. "He's done it again, Carmen. He always sees us through," I said picking up the box and shifting through it. It was heavy, and as I carried it to the kitchen the weight felt good, knowing the heaviness represented a substantial amount of food.

We did not know who left the box, but we were sure of one thing—the Lord always looks out for his own. Our dinner prayer that day was a little extra long and a little extra thankful.

In less than a year, we outgrew our little six-room Jesus house. With twelve living in it and only one bathroom, it became difficult to maintain normal living conditions. As one resident stated, "If you want to use the bathroom, you better have reservations well in advance."

Dwight came in one day and told me, "There's an empty house a few blocks down the street."

We all went to check it out. I liked the house from the outside and went back to call the number indicated on the for-sale sign. The real estate broker introduced himself as Charles.

I asked for the price. He avoided the answer, but rather asked me the purpose for which we wanted it. I told him and he suggested he come over. "I want to see what you're doing," he said.

I took him through our small rented house and gave him an earful of what New Life for Youth was all about. "Let me see your incorporation papers," he said.

"Just a minute; I have them upstairs," I said as I disappeared.

Charles was standing on the back porch, his head down in deep concern.

I hesitated at the foot of the stairs, and then I approached him. "Here are the papers," I said wondering if he was feeling ill.

He looked up. His eyes were red—and moist.

"Victor, I am happy for what you are doing here. You see, I didn't tell you, but I'm a Christian also. God has been dealing with me while we have been going through this place and while you've been telling me what is going on here. I want to help you get the kind of building you need."

"Praise God," I said.

"You'll be hearing from me soon," he said on the way out.

But I didn't. Days went by and there was no word from Charles.

Days turned into weeks and I still waited. No calls, no visits, no word from Charles came.

Meanwhile, I noticed another house for sale nearby—a former doctors' clinic. I called the broker and we made arrangements to tour the place. It was even more ideal than the other building. As I walked through the three-story structure I got excited again. I could picture where the chapel would be, the classroom, and offices—with much more room to house residents seeking help.

Finally, it was time to ask the all-important question, "How much?"

"Thirty-nine thousand," he answered in the usual broker fashion, making it sound like a bargain.

A lump came in my throat. "Wow, that's a lot of money for this house."

"Well, you think about it and let me know," he suggested.

"Yes. In fact, I think I'll pray about this," I said. He looked puzzled at that answer, and we parted company.

I immediately called Charles. When hearing the description of the building, he asked, "When can we go see it?"

"Right now," I answered.

Inside the building, I could see Charles' enthusiasm. "Victor, I really like this place."

We walked through all the rooms and discussed its potential for our purposes. We ended up in the lobby. Suddenly Charles became silent once again as his head bowed. This time I was not concerned but excited. I knew the Holy Spirit was prompting him about something. I had the feeling I was going to enjoy hearing what it was.

He looked up. "How much money do you have for a down payment, Victor?" he asked.

"Nothing, not one penny," I answered.

"Well, that helps. You have to start somewhere and nothing is a beginning," he said taking out a piece of paper. He began writing.

While he jotted down some figures, I began praising the Lord in my mind. "Thank you, Jesus. Thank you, Jesus. Lord, use this man."

"Victor, I think we might be able to get this house. If I can talk the other broker who is handling this house to go half with me on the commission, I'll give you my half which will be $900. If he drops the house entirely, I'll give you all of my commission, which is about $2,000. You can use that towards the down payment."

I left Charles to return to the Jesus house. Our staff and converts began holding special prayer services asking the Lord to remove the other broker.

While we prayed and waited, I drove by the house one afternoon and much to my disappointment the for-sale sign was down. "Oh no, it's been sold. Someone bought the house out from under us," I thought.

I immediately called Charles.

"I'll look into it," he promised. The next day he called, "Your prayers have been answered. The other broker dropped the house because it wasn't selling. We're ready to do business."

"Now to come up with the down payment money," I told Carmen.

"I'm going to give $100.00, Mr. Rider, a Christian layman on the Board of Directors of New Life for Youth told me after finding out about the proposed purchase.

But a few days later we met again and he said, "You know that $100.00 I was going to give you?"

"Yes," I said, wondering what happened to change his mind.

"Well, the Lord spoke to me and made it very clear I should make that $1,000.00 instead of $100.00"

"Praise God," I shouted and leaped for joy inside and out. It seemed that we were praising God continually as events unfolded rapidly to provide the necessary tools for our ministry.

Within weeks we were able to raise the $4,000 needed for the down payment, and the owner lowered the price to $35,000.

The papers were signed, sealed, and delivered. New Life for Youth had a bigger, better, and more usable house for the glory of God and for young people seeking a real home.

315 Dundee Avenue at the intersections of Forest Hills and Semmes was at last ours to occupy. Charles paid me another visit to discuss some business. As he was about to leave he asked, "Where do you live?"

"Carmen and I have an apartment we rent. It's about fifteen minutes from here. We have two little girls, so it's better for us to live away from the house," I explained.

He looked at me seriously and asked, "Do you want to buy a house for you and your family?"

I said, "Oh sure, with the money I've got. Are you kidding?"

"You don't have anything?" he questioned again.

"Not when it comes to money. Nothing is the amount of my bank account."

"Listen, I have to go and check on a house. Why don't you come with me and take a look at it," he suggested.

We drove eight miles or so into a residential section of Richmond. Charles explained that he had bought the house he was taking me to see as an investment.

"I have to check on it because it's vacant right now," he said as he drove the car around a corner. As he did I looked up into the early evening darkness to see the street lamp illuminate one of the green street signs. The name caught my attention—POWELL ROAD.

"Hey, Charles," I exclaimed. "What are you doing taking me to my old neighborhood?"

"What do you mean?"

"Well, back in Brooklyn where I grew up the name of the street we lived on is called Powell Street," I laughed.

He pulled the car into the driveway. I walked toward the house and thought, "Wow. This is beautiful. What a neighborhood. What a lovely house. Someday could Carmen and I own something like this?"

Charles began talking about the house but I didn't hear him. I was too busy dreaming. Then it dawned on me, "Three bedrooms! If only I had the money to buy this. Carmen would flip out. After five years of traveling, she deserves something like this."

I shook myself from daydreaming and dismissed the whole idea. "Charles, you have a real nice house here," I said.

We stood in the middle of the living room. I walked around and when I turned to see Charles, he had gone into his head-down routine.

What now, Charles? I thought with anticipation.

"Ouch! Oh, I am feeling strange again, Victor. I'm beginning to feel the same thing I felt when we first met at the Jesus house," he said.

"Oh yeah, what do you mean?" I questioned.

He put his hand into his pocket and took out a key. "Victor, the Lord is speaking to me. I'm going to give you this house."

"What?" I wasn't able to say anything. "Yes, God wants me to give you this house."

"Charles," I said. "Please don't get carried away." "No. I know what God is doing," he assured me.

Realizing he was dead serious, I couldn't wait to get back to share the news with Carmen. He drove me back to the Jesus house to get my car, and we discussed the details of my taking over the house.

I drove home as fast as possible. As I walked in the door, my tears began to flow down my face.

"Carmen!" I yelled to her inside the door. "You will not believe what has happened. Can you handle this? I've got a surprise."

"Someone is going to pay for the Jesus house," she responded.

"Close your eyes," I said. I pulled the house key from my pocket and put it into her hand. She opened her eyes and looked at it, then at me.

"God just gave us a house," I said so excited I could hardly get the news out of my mouth. I described it as best I could.

We both raised our hands to heaven and began praying in the Spirit.

Carmen, with tears of joy and excitement, said, "Oh Victor, I have been praying and praying for this for some time!"

It was eleven o'clock at night by then, but we got into the car and I drove her to see the place. After inspecting it and as we drove away, I looked at the street sign and said to Carmen, "I can hardly believe it, Honey. Just think, the Lord has brought me from Powell Street to Powell Road. It's almost like a dream."

I explained to Carmen we were getting the house with no down payment, and for the same amount we were paying for rent, we would pay for the mortgage. "As far as I'm concerned, Carmen, it's the same as a gift."

As we drove down Powell Road I thought about the old Victor—a son of evil streets and thanked God once again for delivering me from those streets and putting me on a new road of life—and on POWELL ROAD as well. It was more than the address of our new quarters; it was symbolic of the new life Christ had given me.

The son of evil street had become the son of God and "heir and joint-heir with Jesus Christ."

Driving along Powell Road, Ephesians 2:12–13 came to mind: "*...having no hope, and without God in the world: But now in Christ Jesus ye who sometimes were far off are made nigh by the blood of Christ.*"

# 15

# A VISIT TO THE OLD NEIGHBORHOOD

Several years after my conversion, I had the opportunity to return to my old "Roman Lord" territory with my wife Carmen. We drove down Powell Street and around the neighborhood. I pointed out the old hangouts —the pool hall where we spent many hours, the rooftops where I shot dope, the apartment where our family lived.

As I drove along I spotted a familiar figure. I blew on my horn and hollered, "Little Joe!" I pulled over and got out of the car. It took a moment for him to recognize me.

"Victor! Victor Baby! Hey, what's happening?" He gave me a "high five."

We hugged each other. I turned to introduce Little Joe to Carmen, and I could see that she was surprised at the emotion we still showed for each other after the years of my separation from the neighborhood.

"Wow, man. You're doing all right for yourself," he remarked.

"That's right, Little Joe," I said. "God has been good to me. In fact, he has changed my life. I'm with the Lord now."

He turned away and stared at the sidewalk. I could tell he was either embarrassed or simply indifferent to that statement.

It was apparent that he was still on dope.

"How about you, Joe, how you doin'," I asked wanting to see his reaction.

He explained he had just been released from the penitentiary in Elmira, New York, and was back on the needle. I looked at him and saw a quick reflection of my past. I felt pity and compassion for him and wished I could have put within him what I had.

I stopped my daydreaming and said, "Joe, take a look around you. Who is left in the neighborhood from our old gang? Big Ray is dead."

"Yeah, poor guy," Little Joe said somberly. "He was stabbed twenty-four times all over his body."

"And Indo shot to death by Louis the Knife right near my old apartment." I continued going down the death list.

"Joe," I pleaded. "Get out while you have a chance!" I then asked him to come into the car with Carmen and me to talk further. We drove around the neighborhood streets as I shared more of my testimony. He sat silent and listened. I thought I was getting through. I even offered to take him with me to get away from the area and the life that he was living.

"Victor, you always were smart. You got a good brain." He finally broke his silence. "Man, why don't you stop putting on that religious act and go with me."

"Where," I asked. "What do you mean?"

"Look, I've got this bank all staked out," he said excitedly. "It's all planned, I got a couple of guns; you and I could hit it big. Look, you got the car and the brains, and I got the plan. We could really get into some big money together."

I stopped the car and pulled over. Turning around I looked Little Joe straight in the eyes and said, "Joe, I really feel sorry for you. Maybe you don't believe me, but Jesus Christ has given me all the satisfaction anybody could ever desire. I don't need to do the things that you're doing any longer."

I finished and we drove on again. I saw another familiar face standing on the corner of Christopher Street; the corner that once had been the hottest spot for our gang.

"Beebop!" I yelled from inside the car. He turned and recognized me immediately. A few more of the old crew was around as well and Beebop called them over. I stood with them and once again shared my story. They all looked and listened quietly. When I finished Beebop took a step towards me and offered his hand.

We shook hands firmly. "That's great, Victor. Keep it up. I believe you're headed in the right direction," he said sincerely.

Little did I know that months later he would be killed!

I shook hands with all the guys and introduced them to Carmen. I then suggested to her that it was time to go. I turned once again to Little Joe, "You wouldn't want to change your mind, would you, and come with me?"

"No, I think I will stick around a bit longer," he answered.

"Well, we'll be praying for you, Little Joe," I said as we drove away.

"Yeah, OK," he said with kind of a shrug.

I felt sad that Little Joe would not come my way, but at the same time, I was happy that I was not going his way.

The visit served to convince me further that Christ had delivered me from the gang, from dope, and from all that was once so important to me in my old life.

We left New York and headed toward the New Jersey Turnpike to Virginia. As I drove I began to see it all over again; a picture of the streets of Brownsville and the route the Lord had taken me, almost around the world proclaiming the gospel.

"Carmen, it seems almost like a dream," I mused. The more I thought about it the more chills I felt go up and down my spine. I thought of the countries in which I had the privilege of sharing the "Good News." Places like England, France, Switzerland, Germany, Spain, Lebanon, Chile, Colombia, Ecuador, and other South American countries. Out of the thousands upon thousands of junkies in New York, God came and visited me.

And now, God had brought me to Richmond, Virginia, its prisons, streets, rich, poor, its addicts, and runaways.

"Wow! Carmen. God is taking us to all kinds of people to let them know that He loves them all! We are all His children. You know, Carmen, I love what we are doing."

A favorite scripture came to mind, *"But the God of all grace, who hath called us unto his eternal glory by Christ Jesus, after that ye have suffered a while, make you perfect, stablish, strengthen, settle you"* (1 Peter 5:10).

# 16

# THE MIRACLE GOES ON

The home on Dundee Avenue was now filled to capacity. More importantly, the entire ministry had grown in spite of the struggles we've endured and resistance we have met during our few years of existence. I have watched its expansion and development, and have grown with it.

Contrary to popular belief, the drug problem has not decreased. In fact, it has worsened. Individuals now come to our home, not only strung out on heroin, LSD, cocaine, and speed; but also on crack cocaine and methadone. Unfortunately, methadone is easily available from America's Number One drug pusher—the US government, that dispenses it through legalized clinics across the country. Kicking methadone cold turkey is often two to three times more difficult than withdrawing from heroin.

Not only have we seen an increase in young men coming to us, but now there is also an ever-increasing number of young women. Some are on drugs, some are prostitutes, and others have been simply messed up from poor home environments or other problems. The need to have a separate place for these girls became more and more apparent and a matter of constant prayer on the part of our staff, Carmen, and myself.

But, through much prayer and consideration, God has provided a home for young hurting women to also receive help and healing for their broken lives through our program. Most of the women who come into our center, have survived some of the most horrendous abuse and hurts. The emotional scars are so terrible that many have had to endure extreme oppression in their lives.

One girl, in particular, touched me very deeply every time she would talk about her past. She could not stop crying. She started drinking alcohol when her parents started putting hard liquor in the milk bottle, just to keep her passive. Later on, in her teenage years, she became an alcoholic as well as hooked on crack cocaine and any other thing she could.

It's a tremendous blessing and joy to see Sandy now, living for Jesus and free from her old life. The Women's Home is a dream come true especially when you see all these girls now free and rebuilding their lives.

And yet God had more plans for the expansion of our ministry.

One Friday evening during the time of prayer, sharing, and communion that we have at our home with the staff and the residents of our center, Carmen became burdened and shared what was on her heart. Everyone sat quietly as she enthusiastically related what the Holy Spirit had shown her in a vision.

She saw a place out in the country with rolling hills, plenty of land for running and working, and a place to have cows and grow food. We all sat almost spellbound. My staff and I knew Carmen was not normally given to visions. And, I knew this was too powerful and beautiful to discount. We committed it to the Lord and dismissed the meeting for the evening.

As time went on I let go of the vision from my mind. There were too many other things to think about and too much reality to deal with. Our immediate problem was space. The house for men was filled. With twenty-eight young men, there was not room for recreation, work, study, and other things so important for a smooth running resident ministry such as ours. Yet, I felt helpless to do anything about it. I have always been one for swift action. If things are not progressing I like to do something to move it along. But I could find no solution to our overcrowded conditions. From time to time, I would think about a place in the country where we could send our young Christian converts; away from the many interferences of city life such as the liquor store down the street, a source of constant temptation for them. It was not that we expected to hide them from temptation, for the Christian will always experience some sort of temptation in this life. But in the very early stages of their escape from drugs and sin, we wanted to have them in an environment of peace and quiet.

Suddenly I remembered Carmen's vision. I ran to her, exclaiming, "What about that farm we went to see last year in Spotsylvania County?"

"What farm?" she replied.

"The one that Hawkins told us about," I answered, as a wellspring of faith began to rise within.

I hurriedly called the owner, Mr. Miles. When his wife answered the phone, she said Mr. Miles was not there.

"Do you know where I can reach him?" I asked.

"Yes, he's at our farm. He goes there every Saturday morning to cut hay."

I thanked her and almost before the phone was back on the hook I hollered to Carmen, "Let's go to the farm and talk to Mr. Miles!"

As we drove out there I remembered that it had been a year since we had visited Mr. Miles' place. As we entered, we went up a hill towards a beautiful old colonial house. To me it was breathtaking. Mr. Miles was working on one of his tractors.

We introduced ourselves and told him we were interested in his place. As he showed us around I kept trying to remember how much he was asking for the entire 118-acre farm. I had no money to offer and the more we walked the more I wondered what Carmen and I were doing there. I knew nothing about the real estate business. Then a figure dropped into my mind—$250 per month. I was so engrossed in my thoughts I didn't notice Carmen pulling at my coat. "Honey…Honey," she kept saying, trying to get my attention. "This is the place…the farm…the one I saw in the vision the Lord gave me. Look, the rolling hills, the black cows— it's just as I saw it!"

I looked at Carmen and back over the green spacious acres. We both felt the Holy Spirit confirming that God wanted this for our ministry.

As I shared our burden with Mr. Miles, he asked, "How much can you pay per month?"

I swallowed hard and said, "$250."

He looked at me strangely, not saying anything, but a slight smile graced his face. Then he began asking more questions about our work with troubled youth.

Mr. Miles grew corn, but "Our purpose here," I said, "will be to grow new lives." He turned to me and replied, "You will hear from me within three days."

On the third day, my anxiety got the best of me and I decided to call him, "I want to help you, Victor," Mr. Miles stated. "You can rent for one year and have that time to raise the money for the purchase."

There was much work to be done. The farmhouse had deteriorated so we sent out word to the friends of our ministry, near and far. We shared our burden with them and the future plans for the farm. Many responded and only a few weeks later, fourteen happy young men moved to our farm, as we dedicated it as the New Life for Youth Ranch.

Today our ministry has grown tremendously as we celebrate over forty-five years of reaching the broken and restoring shattered lives. We house, clothe, and feed approximately 200 people on a daily basis. Many have come from a life of hardcore drug addiction ranging from heroin to crack cocaine, and alcoholism. The face of addiction has changed and it not only affects urban areas but the suburbs like never before. In 2017, a small town in West Virginia reported over 27 overdoses in four hours.

The need for New Life for Youth is greater than ever. The young people pour in from the streets, the churches, schools, and some from the gutters of our cities. We minister to them, giving them hope and a chance to live again with a purpose. They stay with us for an entire year as we mentor them through our one-year discipleship program. Our graduates are a testimony to the power of God's grace to change lives. We operate the New Life Ranch in Spotsylvania County, Virginia, for men; The Mercy House in Richmond for troubled women, a Men's Home in Richmond Virginia, and Mercy Moms House which we began after so many years of reaching young women with children. We also operate Celebration Park in Richmond, which is used for vocational training.

Our outreach programs consist of street, prison, schools, and jail ministry along with our many community outreaches.

Celebration Park is a vital part of our rehabilitation/discipleship program for the residents of both the men's and women's programs. It is our 12-acre commercial park that hosts our Thrift Store, Car Wash, Food Bank, Building and Maintenance Department, Call Center, and Auto Shop, and is situated on a highly visible corner in Richmond, Virginia.

New Life for Youth became one of the first to successfully use the model of social enterprise to not only support the ministry, but train young men and women through job readiness programs. It draws people from the community who are also in need. All these small business endeavors empower the students to acquire life skills, an opportunity to share their Christian witness with the community, and use the work experience towards future job opportunities.

One young lady who recently graduated from the program and who had worked in the Thrift Store said to me, "Thank you, Pastor, for New Life. I am leaving here redeemed and with a résumé."

I also like what one young man shared, "Man," he said, "where else can you come buy a piece of furniture, eat a sandwich, and at the same time, get saved?"

Celebration Park is a new concept of outreach. Our students wash the cars and minister to a captive audience, and many people come to Christ. Many with sons, daughters, and friends who are hooked on drugs find out about our ministry and bring their loved ones to the program to receive help. It is also the place where our students receive training for the outside world when they finish the program. The women run the thrift store, the cash register, and they also serve in sales and supervision. One young woman told me recently that she is regaining the trust she had lost from her family and society as a result of her responsibilities at the cash register in her new life. Many of the students find jobs in the community when they graduate as a result of the training they have received while in our program.

Together with my wife, I am also thankful that all my children have been involved in our ministry in various ways, and they are a very important part of New Life.

New Life for Youth continues to be an encouragement not only to the families that we reach on a daily basis but also to the addiction prevention community at large. We have been recognized as one of the most successful organizations in the United States and around the world. Through our partnerships with the police department, schools, and other non-profits; we are able to be a liaison of hope and a model to many other great ministries with the same heart of restoring broken lives.

# 17

# A CHURCH FOR THE TIMES

If someone would have told me when I was on the streets of New York, running with the gangs and dealing dope; that I would be a pastor today, I would have asked them, "What drugs are you on?" But through the faithful prayers of my mother and an available heart, God raised Carmen and me up for such a time as this. Part of the growing miracle throughout the years, is our church, which serves as the family church to all of our students and their families in Richmond, Virginia.

Thirty-four years ago, God spoke to our hearts, telling us to plant a church that will become a spiritual hospital for ministry and continuing outreach, not only for the students in the program but for their families as well. We realized as we affected a son, a daughter, a husband, or a wife who completed the program; they often returned home to non-believing family members and sometimes drug-addicted family members. Some were returning to highly dysfunctional families, which prompted us to reach out to the whole family. We had a vision to see the moms and dads of the students and graduates come to Jesus also.

Today, New Life Outreach International Church is a vibrant living testimony of miracles from all walks of life.

The church operates over 40 ministries and reaches out to the city of Richmond and surrounding counties. The impact in nearby neighborhoods has helped to bring crime down. New Life is truly a light in the darkness. Part of the ongoing cure for those we reach who have come from a life of drug addiction, is the continued discipleship and restoration that church life provides. Many of the graduates from our New Life for Youth program have remained and are now leaders in the church. Our church is filled with living miracles. Most of the members have been saved through our outreach ministries and local evangelism. In fact, hardly a week goes by without someone accepting Christ as their personal Lord and Savior.

The congregation is multicultural, representing people from all over the world. I believe it is a picture of how heaven is going to be, with people from every tongue, nation, and color.

New Life Outreach has been recognized as one of the first churches to break the barrier of segregation on Sundays. Over forty nationalities come together to worship the name of Jesus at our church services.

On August 2003, we moved to our current location, 1005 Turner Road, on approximately 35 acres, with a seating capacity of 1,200 people. With several services throughout the week we have literally seen thousands come to Christ. On any given day of the week the doors are open and lives are changing.

God has given us a vision to plant similar ministries, churches, and homes across America and around the world. Today we have daughter churches in New York City, Huntsville Alabama, and Fredericksburg, Virginia. Internationally we have ministry sites in Peru, Brazil, and the Dominican Republic. We have also launched into Ghana, West Africa, where my daughter, Feliza, and her husband Pastor Angelo Cabrera, together with their two daughters, Annie, and Marisol, planted several churches. My daughter Michelle and her Husband Nick are entrepreneurs and faithful members as well as volunteer in the church together with their children Marielle and Adrian. My son Victor and wife Susana serve in a nearby local church with their beautiful children Jacob, Madeline, and Joanna. Our middle daughter Rosalinda and her husband Carlos continue alongside us, pastoring in our home church and overseeing the New Life for Youth ministry. All three of their children Alana, Gabriel and Victor are involved in the church.

When you surrender to Christ the bible says, "He will save you and your household."[7]

Today Carmen and I consider it a blessing to have our children and grandchildren serving the Lord.

Our vision and calling is to win the lost for Christ and give hope to the hopeless through the love of Christ.

---

7. See Acts 16:31.

# ABOUT THE AUTHOR

Victor Torres was a junkie, drug-pusher, and warlord in Brooklyn's meanest streets. Since his conversion, he has ministered Christ to thousands. He and his wife, Carmen, have traveled to over thirty nations preaching the Good News. Their chief undertaking, however, has been New Life for Youth, which began in 1971 in Richmond, Virginia. This growing work is one of the most respected and largest organizations in the country. Today, New Life for Youth has a ranch in Spotsylvania County, Virginia, which is helping an ever increasing number of hurting young men searching for hope; as well as a home for women with drug-related problems called the Mercy House. House of Hope in Richmond is also a home for recovering men, and Mercy Moms serves women and their children. Victor and Carmen are also the founders and pastors of New Life Outreach International, a fast-growing dynamic church in Richmond, Virginia with over forty nationalities worshiping together.

His story has been made into an award-winning major motion picture called *Victor*.

Visit www.thevictormovie.com to find out how to get your copy.